MICHIGAN AVIATION

MICHIGAN AVIATION

People and Places that Changed History

BARRY LEVINE

Dedication

Sam Levine, U.S. Army Air Force

Frank Quattro, U.S. Marine Corps

Terry Quattro, U.S. Marine Corps

Jim Harshfield, U.S. Navy

Aviation museum volunteers everywhere

Aviation is proof that given the will,
we have the capacity to achieve the impossible.
—Edward V. "Eddie" Rickenbacker

Medal of Honor—1930
National Aviation Hall of Fame—1965
Michigan Aviation Hall of Fame—2011

Contents

Preface

This book's origins go back to 2015, when I began volunteering at Belleville's Yankee Air Museum. The combination of the museum's aircraft, artifacts, and the compelling stories our volunteers and guests have shared with me suggested there was a much larger story to be told. Further reading, site visits, calls, and emails found a treasure trove of photographs, documents, and memorabilia giving new life to Michigan aviation history.

Writing the narrative provided added appreciation of the importance of museums in sharing our common heritage; while my focus is on aviation museums, all history museums are very important. These organizations do a terrific job in telling their part of American history. The time, effort, expertise, and financial support of many volunteers make these museums possible.

So, if you visit an aviation museum, wherever you live, that's a win. Becoming a member at one of these locations would be another win. Sharing that knowledge with friends and family may be the biggest victory of all.

I owe a special note of thanks to my family—Carole, Dan, and Jessica. All provided tons of encouragement and editing assistance over many months of researching and writing. The many people and organizations in the bibliography contributed their own perspectives on various parts of this book which was absolutely critical for getting the job done.

The chapters are in no particular order and can be read independently (other than the concluding chapter covering the Michigan Aviation Hall of Fame). An ongoing goal was to ensure fairness and accuracy throughout the book, while recognizing there are different narratives and perspectives of people and events. Any errors of fact or interpretation are my responsibility.

ONE

○

Norm Ellickson and the *Yankee Lady*

Norm Ellickson—courtesy of Al Hudson.

People are the essence of Michigan's aviation history. One such person is Norm Ellickson, who passed away in November 2020. Ellickson had an impressive aviation resume over decades, both in the private sector and then volunteering at Belleville's Yankee Air Museum. His "capstone" project was restoring and then maintaining the

Yankee Lady—one of the few Boeing B–17G Flying Fortresses that are still flyable anywhere in the world.

Born in the small farming community of Wolverton, Minnesota, Ellickson enrolled in the Spartan School of Aeronautics after high school, becoming a certified aircraft mechanic. He worked on Douglas DC–3s for Wisconsin Central Airlines, served in the Army, and then went to work for North Central Airlines. Airline mergers led to North Central becoming Republic Airlines and then Northwest Airlines. Ellickson was Northwest's night foreman at Detroit Metropolitan Airport in Romulus, ultimately becoming Regional Maintenance Manager until his 1985 retirement.

In addition to his airlines work, Ellickson had a commercial pilot's license, owned several airplanes, and operated Young Airport (now an industrial park), near Jackson Road in Ann Arbor from 1958 to 1962. Ellickson and another early museum volunteer, Lee Koepke, were co-founders of the Detroit Institute of Aeronautics, which evolved into the MIAT College of Technology. Generations of aviation mechanics have been schooled on doing the job "right" with programs established by these men.

Ellickson, member #64 of the Yankee Air Museum, was a key part of the restoration team for the museum's first flyable aircraft, a Douglas C–47; this aircraft was obtained in 1982 and restoration work took about 18 months. The B–17 was acquired in 1986; Ellickson was one of nine people who guaranteed the loan needed to purchase the aircraft.

Ellickson was part of the crew that ferried this aircraft to Michigan. He recalled years later that rolls of duct tape were required to keep the plexiglass nose in place for the flight. This B–17 was manufactured in 1945, but the original World War II design was significantly altered in this aircraft, having been flown by the Coast Guard and then different civilian operators for aerial photography, fire suppression, and crop spraying. It also appeared in the 1970 film *Tora! Tora! Tora!* about Japan's attack at Pearl Harbor.

By the time the museum took possession, much restoration work was required. After nine years of work, the finished aircraft took to the skies in July 1995. Ellickson was a crewmember for that flight. An estimated

120,000 volunteer hours resulted in a beautifully restored aircraft that has won numerous awards.

Ellickson's reputation for quality workmanship helped in obtaining Federal Aviation Administration (FAA) approval for flying paying passengers aboard the restored warbird. The approval and subsequent flights resulted in passengers having a glimpse of what World War II aviation entailed, and as a practical matter, generated fare revenue for offsetting the high operating costs associated with flying vintage aircraft. The *Yankee Lady* has participated in many air shows, veteran's commemorations, and similar events. Ellickson and his wife Karen often travelled together with the B-17; Karen managed the airborne gift shop, and Norm served as crew chief.

Obtaining parts became a constant concern as Flying Fortress production ceased in 1945. Ellickson was constantly on the lookout for these items, actively participating in a B-17 co-op program, where operators exchange information about parts availability. A sample transaction included swapping a starboard wing oil tank for a plexiglass nose.

The *Yankee Lady* is always a popular attraction wherever it appears. Interviewed in 2013 at a New Jersey air show, Ellickson noted that former bomber crew members often attend events featuring the *Yankee Lady* with varying emotions: "I've had a lot of guys come up and touch the airplane and literally walk away crying. Sometimes, they'll stand back and won't go near it—their last flight was bailing out of a B-17 over Germany."

Ellickson received numerous awards such as the Charles Taylor Master Mechanic Award from the FAA, honoring mechanics with over fifty years of outstanding service. He received a "Special Achievement Award" from the International Council of Airshows at the 2014 ICAS Chairman's Banquet.

Norm Ellickson's drive to support our aviation legacy could be summarized in his own words: "We'll keep the *Yankee Lady* flying as long as humanly possible—we owe our veterans nothing less." As one would expect, he received many glowing tributes about his dedication, knowhow, willingness to share information, and all-around generous nature. A sample follows:

- ICAS host Rob Reider: "Norm has earned this recognition for the passion he brings to his work with warbirds and the people who maintain and fly them...For all the good work he and the Yankee Air Museum have done to help keep America's vintage military aircraft flying and accessible to the public, we owe him our gratitude."
- Restoration team for *The City of Savannah* B-17 at the National Museum of the Mighty 8th Air Force, Pooler, Georgia: "Norm provided sage advice, some important parts, and sincere friendship when we needed it."
- Yankee Air Museum's founder Dennis Norton: "No one could replace what Norm did for the organization over its entire history... He is one of the never to be forgotten pillars of the Yankee Air Museum."

There is no doubt that Norm Ellickson's contributions to the Michigan aviation world were enormous. And, there is no doubt Ellickson is one example of many outstanding men and women that have selflessly given of themselves to Michigan aviation museums. We are all better off for their work.

TWO

○

Selfridge—Quite the Spot in Aviation History

Selfridge-based P-40 over Detroit, circa 1940—courtesy of Selfridge Military Air Museum.

Michigan's Selfridge Air Base, in Harrison Township and adjacent to Lake St. Clair, has contributed to aviation history for decades. This chapter focuses on two very compelling stories—the history of the base as well as some of the aviators who served there.

Selfridge's roots go back to Detroit native Henry Joy, who led an investor group in buying Packard Motor Car Company in 1902; Joy later became Packard's president, and then board chairman. One of Packard's efforts during World War I was developing Liberty aircraft engines. As these engines needed flight testing, Packard acquired land in Harrison Township, which was initially named Joy Aviation Field.

This land was first leased and was then purchased by the federal government for $190,000; nearby Detroit's industrial might was a selling point. Joy Aviation Field was renamed Selfridge Field after Lt. Thomas Selfridge—the first U.S. military person killed in a motorized airplane crash. That September 1908 flight occurred in Virginia and was piloted by Orville Wright, who was seriously injured in the incident.

Selfridge was one of nine U.S. military airfields when the first aircraft to fly into the base—a Curtiss JN-4 "Jenny"—arrived in July 1917. During World War I, pilot trainees were sent to Selfridge for a three-week aerial gunnery course, firing at stationery and moving targets from the air.

Selfridge's early days had many challenges. Personnel were quarantined in late 1918 as that year's global pandemic was severe in nearby communities. In a fifty-year anniversary story in the *Detroit News*, veterans remembered that fires were built at the end of the runway for night flights as there were no landing lights. One of the mechanics remembered, "Between the flu and flying, we had a lot of funerals."

Construction was difficult as some areas were below lake level and prone to flooding; material and equipment were brought in by barge and rail lines. When the Clinton River overflowed its banks in March 1918, local residents boarded soldiers in their homes. (Selfridge returned the favor in 1964 by providing shelter to residents whose housing was damaged or destroyed by tornadoes). The area benefited from the 1925 bombing of ice jams on the Clinton River by Selfridge aircraft. A seawall was built, underground drainage pipes and a spillway were constructed between the river and the lake to resolve these problems and to avoid additional ice jam bombing.

After World War I, Selfridge was used for training mechanics and as a gunnery school. A series of air races and shows were held in the 1920s and 1930s, such as the John Mitchell Trophy Race. A 1923 *Detroit Free Press* article described seventy-five "aeroplanes" that participated and "thrilled thousands." Airplane rides were offered on a lottery basis; tickets cost $1 each and were available at local drug stores and hotels. These events were more than a spectacle for the fans—they helped build citizen support of aviation.

The interwar years between World War I and World War II saw Selfridge personnel participating in drills and exercises involving communications, gunnery, high altitude flying, navigation, and aerial tactics. For example, a 1936 exercise involved Selfridge-based aircraft defending Ft. Knox, Kentucky, against bombers from Virginia's Langley base. All of these skills were put to use in World War II.

During World War II, Selfridge was primarily an Army Air Force training base and experienced the difficult race relations of the era. Some African American airmen who had initially trained at Tuskegee Army Air Field in Alabama were then assigned to Selfridge. Discrimination was common—for example, there was a whites-only policy for the Selfridge Officer's Club. After their Selfridge training, some fighter squadrons were transferred overseas and excelled in combat operations in North Africa and Italy.

One medium-bomber squadron, however, ran into many difficulties with racism and lack of support and was transferred to a base in Kentucky and then to Freeman Field in Indiana. At Freeman Field, a number of officers were charged with insubordination for not accepting a segregated officers club on base—one of whom was Coleman Young, future Mayor of Detroit.

In a non-traditional assignment, Selfridge was home to a Signal Pigeon Company, used for carrying messages in World War II. As in World War I, signal pigeons may have been the only means of communication for combat units in isolated areas where conventional communications were impossible.

Selfridge was involved in various Cold War missions after World War II: In 1948, a flight of Lockheed P-80 single-seat jet aircraft departed Selfridge to complete the first west-to-east jet crossing of the Atlantic. Multiple stops were required, and the mission was a success. Nike air defense missiles were installed at Selfridge and other metro Detroit locations beginning in 1955. During the 1962 Cuban Missile crisis, Selfridge's F-106 Delta Dart fighter aircraft were on five-minute alert status. Pilots and maintenance personnel slept in hangers as part of their job with Air Defense Command.

1963 saw humanitarian missions such as the delivery of medical supplies to Honduras from Selfridge. The doctor in charge of a medical clinic in a remote area of Honduras traveled to the U.S. to obtain medical supplies but there was no available transportation. Selfridge personnel read of the situation, obtained the required approvals, and with air crews from other bases, flew needed supplies to Honduras.

In 1967, the base was used as a staging area for 82nd and 101st Airborne troops during civil unrest in Detroit. These soldiers were flown in from Fort Bragg and Fort Campbell to help maintain order.

On July 1, 1971, Selfridge became Selfridge Air National Guard (ANG) Base, described in a press release as the biggest military turnover to a reserve unit as of that time. Michigan's Air National Guard has its own very distinguished history, beginning in 1925 with local aviation people meeting for drills in a Detroit Police municipal garage. An Observation Squadron assigned to Selfridge was authorized in May 1926—making Michigan the fifth state to have a Federally recognized National Guard air unit. After using a temporary field at Rouge Park in Detroit, the Guard moved to Detroit City Airport in 1928 and 1929, then to a hangar at Wayne County (now Metro) Airport in October 1930.

ANG units, as with their Air Force predecessors, have been an integral component to Michigan and U.S. history. Operation Baby Lift, conducted in 1975, had flights from Chicago to Detroit with refugees who escaped North Vietnam's invasion of South Vietnam. Armed combat patrols were flown over metro Detroit after the September 2001 terrorist attacks. Fighter aircraft were on alert twenty-four hours a day, seven days a week to deal with threats. Selfridge units airlifted troops and equipment to Iraq in 2003 and were deployed to Afghanistan from 2011 to 2012.

Civilian as well as defense needs were met; Selfridge was used as a FEMA storage facility in the Flint water crisis in 2016. During the

height of the COVID-19 pandemic in 2020, Selfridge aircraft participated in flyovers of various Michigan health facilities as a "Thank You"
to Michigan health care workers.

Other Military Units

Naval reserve squadron VP 93, known as the "Executioners," flew propeller driven, four-engine Lockheed P-3 Orions from Selfridge until the
end of the Cold War; one of this squadron's aircraft is displayed at Selfridge Military Air Museum. Missions might include shadowing Soviet
Union submarines or monitoring oil spill effects in the Gulf of Mexico.
Drug interdiction missions were common, looking for fishing trawlers
that were not followed by sea gulls, suggesting fish was not the cargo.
If suspicious activities were observed, the Coast Guard would be advised.

The Coast Guard moved to Selfridge in 1966 and has a primary area
of responsibility of over 1,000 miles of Great Lakes shoreline. Aircrews
fly over 3,000 hours per year, conducting about 350 search and rescue
missions. Since its commissioning in 1966, Air Station Detroit has saved
over 1,450 lives and has assisted on many other rescue efforts.

Aviators

Of course, aviation units need aviators, and a long list of distinguished
aviators have served at Selfridge. Selfridge has been known as the
"Home of the Generals." Well over 100 airmen who served at Selfridge
became generals in the Army Air Force and/or the Air Force. Three
of them—Carl Spaatz, Curtis LeMay, and George Brown—went on to
become Air Force Chiefs of Staff.

General Carl A. Spaatz was appointed the first Air Force Chief of
Staff in 1947. Before World War II, he led the 1st Pursuit Group from its
Texas base to Selfridge and became the Group's commanding officer.
When then-Major Spaatz transferred from Selfridge to Langley in 1924,
local newspapers commented on how highly respected he was by officers
and enlisted personnel.

General Curtis LeMay was appointed Air Force Chief of Staff in
1961 and was instrumental in developing the Strategic Air Command,
a linchpin of our national defense triad during the Cold War. In about

1930, 2nd Lt. LeMay was based at Selfridge and flew a biplane through a hangar. It is unknown if this was on a dare or a bet; the net result was a $50 fine from the Commanding Officer—big money in those days.

General George S. Brown was Air Force Chief of Staff in 1973–1974 and became Chairman of the Joint Chiefs of Staff from 1974–1978. Brown was commander of the 56th Fighter Interceptor Wing at Selfridge in the early 1950s and served in both Korea and Vietnam.

In addition to the future military leaders, a wide range of men and women who served at Selfridge have made contributions to aviation history—a very small sample includes:

Byron Jones became the first commander of the pilot training facility on base in 1917. Earlier in his career, he was the first U.S. airman to see combat—against Pancho Villa in Mexico. "This will be a strict military school," then-Captain Jones said in an *Aviation Journal interview in* 1917, "regular Army officers will be in charge and our greatest desire will be to train the students as quickly as possible and at the same time to instill strict military discipline into them." Later in life, he submitted on behalf of the Army the patent application for the "Jeep" (Jones did not design the Jeep, but did hold a number of aviation-related patents).

Brig. General Frank Lackland—As a Major on base during 1918, Lackland served at the School of Aerial Gunnery. In his distinguished aviation career, Lackland served in a variety of capacities before retiring in 1942. The Indoctrination Division, Air Training Command, in San Antonio, Texas, was named Lackland AFB in his honor in July 1947.

Captain Eddie Rickenbacker, America's top World War 1 air ace and a Medal of Honor recipient, was part of the 94th Pursuit (nicknamed the "Hat in the Ring") Squadron at Selfridge after World War I, which arrived in 1919.

Colonel Russell Meredith earned a Distinguished Flying Cross in 1923, when he flew a doctor to Beaver Island in Lake Michigan in hazardous winter conditions when a resident needed medical assistance.

Charles Lindbergh was temporarily stationed at Selfridge Air Field. Arriving in 1924 for tactical training, he then completed reserve training in 1927 at Selfridge. The "Spirit of St. Louis" was hangered at Selfridge while Lindbergh completed his service obligation during World War II.

Lt. Colonel Boyd Wagner was assigned to the 27th Pursuit Squadron with the 1st Pursuit Group at Selfridge. Wagner became the first U.S. ace in World War II in action over the Philippines in December 1941.

Major Urban "Ben" Drew—A Detroit native, Drew became the first pilot to shoot down two enemy jet aircraft in a single mission while flying a propeller-driven P-51 Mustang (named "The Detroit Miss") in World War II. Drew became the first assistant adjutant general for air for the Michigan National Guard, helping organize the Michigan ANG after the Air Force became a separate military service.

General Daniel James served in the 477th Bomb Squadron that trained at Selfridge during World War II, he then went on to fly combat missions in Korea and Vietnam. James became the Air Force's first African American four-star general.

General Benjamin O. Davis, Jr. served at Selfridge in 1943 before being transferred to Italy and flying sixty combat missions in Europe in World War II. Davis, a man of incredible drive and determination, was shunned all four years at West Point (no one would room, eat, or speak to him unless it was official business) because he was African American. He was the only black cadet in the class of 1936; he became the first African American general in the Air Force in 1954. President Clinton presented Davis with his fourth star in a 1998 ceremony.

Lt. Aleda Lutz, from Freeland (near Saginaw) was a nurse who was stationed at Selfridge, before being accepted as a flight nurse, which had very difficult specialized training. Lutz participated in battle campaigns in Tunisia, Italy, and France, was awarded the Distinguished Flying Cross, but was killed in a plane crash in France in 1944.

Lt. Col. Alexander Jefferson—From Detroit, Jefferson was a Tuskegee Airman during World War II and served at Selfridge before being sent overseas. He flew P-51 Mustangs over Europe before being shot down. After the war, Jefferson co-founded the Detroit Tuskegee Airman Museum and was a long-time educator in Detroit's public schools. He wrote his auto-biography, *Red Tail Captured, Red Tail Free: Memoirs of a Tuskegee Airman and POW* in 2005.

General Charles de Gaulle—The leader of the Free French (and later President of France) arrived in August 1945 to visit French airmen training at Selfridge. Archives in the Mt. Clemens Library noted that after greeting his troops, de Gaulle remarked:

"I especially wanted to stop at Selfridge Field, this important American Air base, where the French Cadets receive the finishing touch to their training, to show my interest in their young students and to bring the thanks of France to the American people and their American Air Force for their help they have extended to us during the war, towards the formation of our crews and the rebuilding of our air force."

Colonel Francis Gabreski—Gabreski was one of our top air aces (five or more enemy aircraft destroyed) in World War II and then commanded the 56th Fighter Group at Selfridge before assignment to Korea during that conflict. Including Gabreski, five Korean War aces served at Selfridge and became known as the "MiG killers." MiG15s were jets fighters designed by the Soviet Mikoyan-Gurevich Design Bureau, which were sometimes flown by Soviet pilots.

Colonel Dave Schilling—Schilling was the commanding officer of the fighter group completing the 1948 trans-Atlantic crossing. Always an innovator, Schilling dealt with problematic winter weather issues, such as stopping aircraft on snow-covered runways. Schilling had a jet engine mounted on the back of a hydraulic lift; the heat from the blast blew off snow and melted ice on the runway.

Lt. Commander Lonnie Mixon and Lt. Jack Rittichier—In November 1966, a Coast Guard helicopter, flown by Mixon and Rittichier, rescued eight sailors stranded on the German freighter in a very severe Lake Huron storm. Mixon received a Distinguished Flying Cross and Rittichier earned an Air Medal for this rescue. These flyers then served in Vietnam; Rittichier became the only Coast Guard aviator killed in Vietnam on a rescue attempt. Selfridge's Coast Guard hangar was dedicated in his memory in 1969.

Lt. Col. Don "Digger" O'Dell—During the Vietnam war, O'Dell ("Digger" was his call sign) was shot down in 1967 and captured by the North Vietnamese. O'Dell and other POWs used a variety of mind exercises to cope with this experience, such as estimating his cell's dimensions and the distance paced each day. "At one point, I was certain I had walked from Hanoi to Mt. Clemens." Repatriated home in 1973,

O'Dell became Selfridge's Public Affairs director from 1975–1990; in his view: "I am very proud to have served with such dedicated, patriotic, and proud Americans in the camps of North Vietnam. I only hope that we as Americans will not forget those who made the ultimate sacrifice."

Brig. General Rolf Mammen—As of February 2021, General Mammen is the Commander of the 127th Wing at Selfridge. On September 11, 2001, Mr. Mammen was the First Officer of a United Airlines flight from London to New York's Kennedy Airport (he was then a full time United employee while serving in the Air National Guard). The aircraft was diverted to Halifax; First Officer Mammen spent most of the rest of the flight guarding the cockpit door with a fire axe while his fellow pilots flew the aircraft. Mammen was fully prepared to use the axe if the door was breached.

Not all personnel in Selfridge's history have been heroic. Colonel William Colman was the center of a particularly ugly incident in May 1943. Colman, one of the senior officers on base, had requested a driver late at night. When Private William McRae, who was African American, arrived, Colman shot and wounded him. Colman was court martialed and reduced to the rank of captain.

Going Forward

Selfridge is now home to the 127th Air Wing, which was formed in 1996. Units from all five military branches are on site. The Wing's "Fact Sheet" notes "the 127th Wing is one of the most complex units in the U.S. Air Force. As a component of the Michigan Air National Guard, the Wing has a dual state and federal role and stands ready to serve both at home and abroad." Selfridge Air Base is also home to Army, Navy, Marine, and Seabee units and a U.S. Customs & Border Patrol team.

Selfridge Military Air Museum

Visitors to Selfridge can see history commemorated at the Selfridge Military Air Museum, formed in 1975 by the Michigan Air Guard Historical Association. The first Selfridge Museum director (1976–1996) was Col. Robert Stone. The director in 2020 was Chief Master Sergeant (retired) Wayne Fetty who supplied the "quite the spot" quote in the chapter title. Fetty has moved on to another position at the Eisenhower Center on base; the new director is Army veteran Steve Mrozek. The Museum has forty aircraft on display, commemorating years of aviation history and showcasing Selfridge's role in defending America.

THREE

___O___

Aircraft Restoration

Camel at the Air Zoo—courtesy of the author.

V isitors to any of Michigan's aviation museums can see, close up, some beautifully restored aircraft. This chapter covers the restoration of three such aircraft: a family project to build a Sopwith F.1 Camel, which was finished by Portage's Air Zoo Aerospace & Science Museum, and work on a Consolidated PB4Y-2 Privateer, and Boeing B-52 Stratofortress by Belleville's Yankee Air Museum.

Sopwith Camel

The Air Zoo has on display a hand-built reproduction Sopwith F.1 Camel fighter, one of the most famous aircraft of World War I. Long-time Michigan resident Gordon Beatty, various Beatty family members, and the Air Zoo's restoration staff worked for years on this project.

Camels have a remarkable place in aviation history—it was a state-of-the-art aircraft manufactured by a British company formed by Sir Thomas Sopwith in December 1916. Only thirteen years had passed since the Wright brothers' first powered, controllable flight at Kitty Hawk. As always, aviation technology progressed quickly.

Camels shot down almost 1,300 enemy aircraft during World War I, more than any other Allied fighter. Almost 5,500 were built, designed for a one-man crew and armed with two Vickers 7.7 mm machine guns that were synchronized to fire through, without shooting off, the propeller.

The name "Camel" was derived from the hump-shaped cover over the machine guns, which were mounted side-by-side in front of the cockpit. Flying a Camel was a high-risk proposition; the forward center of gravity made them challenging to fly, the wood and fabric construction and unprotected fuel tank posed a fire risk, and limited pilot training did not help.

Canada's most highly decorated soldier, William Barker, was a World War I fighter pilot and indirectly became part of the restoration story. His Camel (#B6313) became World War I's single most successful fighter aircraft (forty-six enemy aircraft destroyed) until its October 1918 retirement. Barker was awarded the Victoria Cross, the United Kingdom's highest military honor, in October 1918. Flying alone, he came under attack by fifteen German aircraft. Seriously injured, he downed four enemy aircraft and drove off the remainder before crash landing behind Allied lines.

Back in the U.S., the Homer Beaty family was on a path leading to building a reproduction of Bill Barker's Camel. Indiana native Beaty was an Army machine gunner during World War I. Enlisting in 1917, he left for France with the 16th Regiment, one of the first American units to arrive in Europe. He was in action at the first battle for American soldiers at Cantigny.

Injured in May 1918, he was awarded a Silver Star; then he fought in the Battle of Soissons, suffering a second and more serious injury in July 1918. He recuperated in France and returned home in April 1919 with two walking canes. Pain was a constant, finally resulting in the amputation of his leg above the knee. Beaty became a barber and passed away in 1971.

One of Homer's children was A. Gordon Beatty (everyone called him Gordon). The Army added a second "t" in Gordon's World War II paycheck, which remained for succeeding generations of the family. Beatty loved flying from a very young age; as a young boy he drew an accurate image of a "Curtiss Hell Diver" (an early version of a Navy dive bomber) and planned to buy a balsa version of this aircraft once he saved 35 cents.

One of Beatty's heroes was Eddie Rickenbacker, America's top ace of World War I and a Medal of Honor recipient. Beatty was a B-24 mechanic in England and may have seen or met Rickenbacker, who toured U.S.A.A.F. bases in World War II. Rickenbacker's visit may have further prompted an interest in World War I aviation, along with his father's heroics and subsequent life challenges.

Once he returned from England, Beatty got to thinking about honoring the World War I veterans—and thus his father—by building a reproduction Camel. Family members are uncertain about the Camel project's exact origin. Son Rob thought the uniqueness of Camels in North America was a factor. Daughter Lynn thought it might be the aircraft's historical significance. Wife Martha believed the challenge of building a reproduction aircraft was irresistible. Regardless of the reason, the aircraft reproduction world owes a debt of gratitude to Martha Beatty for her essential support of the project.

Work began in the early 1950s. The blueprints Beatty followed are from Clayton and Shuttleworth, a British business that manufactured Camels for Sopwith. Gordon did most of the work himself. Rob assisted with the tires; Martha and Lynn sewed the linen onto the fuselage. This material was obtained from Ireland and was the same as the fabric that had been installed on production aircraft.

The pilot's seat and the rotary Clerget engine were authentic. Beatty drove to Chicago to pick up two functioning machine guns. As one would expect, Beatty owned a wide range of equipment and tools for making parts, including a small foundry. A constant goal was to build the Camel to factory specifications.

Beatty spent at least thirty-five years on the project. It was a labor of love, and with no real time constraint for completion (he was working, had family obligations, and was a ham radio operator), the plane started out being built in the family's basement in Detroit. The family and the airplane relocated to California before moving back to Michigan. Once the plane grew too large for the basement, it moved to the second stall of the garage. Lynn said she "doesn't recall EVER not having the plane in the garage." The Camel was part of a subsequent move to Manistee across the street from Blacker Airport, where it was housed in an airport hangar. Once, the family dog got out of the house and knew right where to find Beatty—in the hangar.

The Camel was loaned in 2000 to the Air Zoo. The lead restoration person was Boyd Naylor—a volunteer who worked for twelve years on the project. Naylor built many of the wing components such as the aileron pulleys and hinges and the fittings to connect the wing struts to the wing. Aviation-grade spruce and ash woods were used in the wings and mahogany was used around the cockpit.

As did Beatty, the Air Zoo insisted on extremely high standards of workmanship. Ryan Knapp, who worked at the Air Zoo as a teenager and who is now an Air Force helicopter pilot, recalls a team effort to install the wings at "just the right angle" so that the wing struts fit properly. Parts of the wings were left uncovered so visitors could see Naylor's impressive handiwork.

Gordon Beatty passed away in 1994 and did not live to see the finished product; that said, thousands of people get to see the Camel every year visiting the Air Zoo.

There are a few follow-up items to bring the story to its conclusion. William Barker returned to Canada, had a variety of business interests, and served as the first president of the Toronto Maple Leafs hockey team. Sadly, Barker was killed in an airplane crash in March 1930.

Barker's nephews, Joe and Rick, visited the Air Zoo in 2003, meeting with Rob Beatty and his daughter Alison (who later became the leader of the Willow Run Tribute Rosies at the Yankee Air Museum). This must have been an emotional moment for all. Joe noted that the Camel was far more complex than he anticipated; both of the Barkers found the cockpit very cramped.

The Sopwith company ran into financial difficulty after World War I. Test pilot Harry Hawker, along with other investors, bought Sopwith's assets and formed what became Hawker Aircraft Limited. Hawker produced some of the most important aircraft in history including the Hawker Hurricane—a key R.A.F. workhorse in the 1940 Battle of Britain.

In contemporary times, fans of the late Charles Schulz "Peanuts" cartoon will remember Snoopy's imaginary dogfights against the Red Baron. Snoopy always imagined his doghouse as a Sopwith Camel. When asked about the origins of Snoopy's aviator role, Schulz said the inspiration came from his son's interest in making airplane models. Schulz drew a helmet on Snoopy after seeing one of these models and "suddenly got the idea for it."

Yankee Air Museum

The Yankee Air Museum in Belleville, Minnesota, has a long history of working on ambitious, challenging restoration projects. Two such projects included extensive work on a Consolidated PB4Y-2 Privateer (the Navy's variant of a B-24 Liberator) and a Boeing B-52 Stratofortress bomber. These restoration efforts were independent of each other.

Consolidated PB4Y-2 Privateer

The museum's aircraft was number 527 (740 were manufactured), and it was delivered to the Navy in August 1945. Consolidated modified the B-24 design by extending the nose to hold electronic gear, substituting a single-boom for the Liberator's twin-boom tail design, removing the ball turret, and adding a second top turret on the fuselage. Pratt & Whitney 14-cylinder engines were installed, suitable for lower altitude Navy missions.

Privateer missions included patrols over the Pacific in the waning days of World War II and dropping flares off of the Korean shore to illuminate Communist infiltrators during the Korean War. The French military used Privateers against Egypt in the 1956 Suez conflict. In April 1950, the Soviet Union shot down a Privateer on an electronic reconnaissance mission over the Baltic Sea.

The museum's aircraft was used by the Navy and Coast Guard for training and search and rescue missions and had been based in locations such as Hawaii, Wake, and Guam. Sold by the Navy in late 1957, it was flown by various civilian operators such as Hawkins and Powers Aviation in Greybull, Wyoming. Hawkins and Powers obtained the Privateer in 1969, using it as an aerial firebomber.

This aircraft crash-landed near Port Hardy, British Columbia, in August 1975 after running out of fuel. The Privateer slid into the Pacific Ocean in shallow water and was heavily damaged—it was later hauled out by a bulldozer. The aircraft was neglected for six years before it was ultimately acquired by a U.S. based company, cut into pieces, and transported to Michigan in eleven truckloads. These assorted parts were donated to the Yankee Air Museum in 1987. Some referred to it as the "Scrap-a-teer" given its poor condition, and at the time there was little optimism the Privateer could be salvaged.

However, dedicated effort by the late George Whitfield and a restoration team had the Privateer standing on its landing gear in nine months. For many years, the aircraft was displayed in an outdoor area adjacent to the museum, with Michigan's climate taking a toll on the airframe. In 2015, the Privateer was moved into the remaining 144,000 square feet of the Willow Run Bomber Plant, which had been obtained by the museum.

Restoration work is ongoing, and has generously been supported by the Riley Foundation. Detroit native George Riley, who served as a radar- and sonarman in the Navy, flew on PB4Ys in the early 1950s. Returning to Michigan, Riley founded Clover Television in 1952,

Privateer—courtesy of the Yankee Air Museum Privateer Restoration Team.

which later became Clover Technologies and was sold in 1998. George and his wife Dolores Riley established the Riley Foundation, supporting charitable causes including funding the Privateer's restoration. George Riley passed away in 2018.

While many of the original work crew have passed away, the museum continues to draw in new volunteers who enjoy working on this aviation treasure. Crew chief Joe Amend heads a team of eighteen volunteers who face many challenges with this project. Logistics is an issue, as most of the work is done in Willow Run Airport Hangar F6, which is located several miles away from the original Bomber Plant. Hangar F6 is crowded, unheated, and not airconditioned.

New parts are simply not available as Privateers were last manufactured in 1945. The Privateer team sometimes barters with other museums, aircraft operators, and aviation businesses to buy, sell, and trade parts.

If a part is not available, it may be recreated by finding related photographs and drawings and then engineering the item. As an example, the team is building a replica of the Engineering and Research Corporation bow turret originally installed on Privateers. Work included obtaining a plexiglass hemisphere the approximate size of the ERCO design, building reinforcements and mountings, and cutting the plexiglass to fit the .50 caliber machine guns used on Privateers.

Tires were another challenge. The team decided to use a polyure-thane filling compound to enhance appearance and functionality. The tires were removed from the aircraft, sent to an outside vendor, filled, and remounted on the Privateer. The main landing gear tires now have over 1,700 pounds of foam each, allowing the Privateer to be properly displayed and moved if needed.

The project's overarching goal is to ensure a beautifully restored aircraft matching a Consolidated-built original as closely as possible. Reference materials about B-24s/Privateers are extensively used for accuracy. The National Naval Air Museum in Pensacola, Florida, provided assistance for building the bow turret mount, rebuilding the turret's inside, and in casting the blister turret plexiglass. The extensive project list requires teamwork, ingenuity, and creativity, and engineering, welding, metal working, painting, carpentry, and electrical skills.

The final paint scheme for the Privateer will closely match the Navy configuration of George Riley's aircraft as a fitting tribute for his many contributions to this project. The team, as is typical for restoration teams everywhere, are dedicated to the task. Volunteer John Grudzien notes that everyone on the team is "plane crazy." Volunteer Barry Tyrell mentioned that he wants to show appreciation for the men and women, including his father, whose World War II service maintained our freedoms. Of course, when the restoration team meets someone who had direct ties to a PB4Y-2 or a B-24 Liberator, the experience is unbelievable.

Boeing B-52 Stratofortress

Boeing's B-52s have a long and distinguished U.S. Air Force history. First flown in 1952, the B-52's missions have included nuclear deterrence, conventional ordnance platform, and cruise missile delivery. These aircraft are expected to continue flying for decades more with ongoing avionics and engine updates.

B-52D Serial Number 55-0677 was manufactured in Wichita, Kansas, and delivered to the Air Force in August 1957. Often referred to as "677," this aircraft flew over 600 combat missions during the Vietnam war from Guam, Okinawa, and U-Tapao Royal Thai Naval Airfield in

A B-52 work party—courtesy of Susan Torrible.

Thailand. 677 participated in Operation Linebacker II, an intense bombing campaign against North Vietnam that led to the Paris Peace Accords in January 1973. After combat operations ceased in Vietnam, bombing in Laos continued and 677 is believed to be the last B-52 to bomb Laos in February 1973.

After Vietnam, 677 returned to the U.S. In 1983, it was flown from Carswell Air Force Base in Texas to Willow Run on loan from the National Museum of the United States Air Force. On Memorial Day 1984, 677 was dedicated as a permanent memorial to all aircrews who lost their lives in Southeast Asia. For years, most visitors to the museum would notice a B-52D, parked in a fenced off area at Willow Run Airport. Of course, it would be hard to miss, with its 185-foot wingspan and a 40-foot-tall tail.

While there are no known records indicating battle damage while over Vietnam, nature was not so kind to 677. Over the years, the fuselage suffered from corrosion and began deteriorating. By 2014, the deterioration reached a point where scrapping 677 may have become necessary. Ralph Koehler, the museum's restoration manager, called Joe Provost, who had served as a B-52 crew chief at U-Tapao, and asked if 677 was salvageable.

Provost contacted museum members Bob Bailey and Nick Consiglio who evaluated the airframe and determined that 677 could be restored. Provost and Consiglio had a special connection to 677, as they worked on it in their Air Force days in Thailand during the Vietnam War; Bailey had served in Thailand as well.

Work began in 2015. Provost, Bailey, and Consiglio—along with Air Force veterans Luke Noble and Dave Barnhart—coordinated the ongoing restoration efforts throughout the year. They scheduled work to be completed, equipment needed, and determined if any special materials or tooling were required.

Two additional teams have been involved in this work on 677. One team included students at nearby MIAT College of Technology, in Canton, Michigan. These students worked on many aspects of the project while earning college credit and receiving expert aircraft restoration knowledge. Real-life job skills were provided to these young men and women, as well as offering them a firsthand history lesson.

The second team was composed of volunteers from any branch of the service who'd been were permanently stationed or on temporary duty at U-Tapao during the Vietnam War. These "work parties" are hosted by Provost, Bailey, and Consiglio. The first such work party was first held in 2016. Attendees come from many different states to work on the restoration, as well as enjoying camaraderie with fellow veterans and sharing a few war stories.

The teams have made considerable progress over the last few years. Restoration work has included reskinning both wing roots and all 16 engine cowlings, repairing the right-wing leading edge and various cracks and corrosion in multiple fuselage locations, restoring four engine nacelles and most of the bomb bay doors, plus various mechanical tasks.

Future plans include restoring the left-wing leading edge, reskinning the majority of the left-wing underside, ongoing corrosion repair, general maintenance, and installing the restored engine nacelles. Another goal for 677 is restoring the original Southeast Asia black and camo paint configuration.

Work party participants have provided many comments about why they spend their time, money, and effort on this project. Brad Beall was a tail gunner on 677 when it was based in both Guam and U-Tapao. Beall lives in Illinois and traveled to Willow Run to work on 677, noting, "It's just so cool to be able to work on the same aircraft I flew on during the war."

Consiglio, who uses the same tool bag as in his U-Tapao days, noted: "We have U-Tapao veterans and their families from all over the nation, at their expense, come to Willow Run to partake in her restoration. Many of these vets never touched an airplane when they served but are happy to work their hearts out." Bailey commented: "We need to preserve what we can of aviation history and the memory of all the men and woman who came before us."

2020 presented new challenges—the coronavirus limited opportunities for planned maintenance—also, the B-52's display area from 1983–2020 was being repurposed by Wayne County's Airport Authority (Willow Run's managing agency), so a new location was needed for this aircraft.

Museum leadership decided to move 677 to the east side of the Willow Run complex, in front of the Yankee Air Museum's Roush Aeronautics Center, now under construction. The Center will house the museum's flyable aircraft. Concrete pads for the landing gear were poured in August 2020, and Nebraska's Worldwide Aircraft Recovery moved 677 about one mile down a taxiway to its new home that September.

Worldwide brought out new tires, jacks, and tow bars, hoisted the B-52, put on special tires, and towed the B-52 to its new location. As some of the move was over grass, work crews moved aluminum planks in front of the wheels; this process was continually repeated as the B-52 was moved. The entire process took several days to complete. Once on its new concrete pads, the B-52 was raised on jacks, the original tires reinstalled, and 677 was lowered into place.

Future visitors to the Roush Aeronautics Center will be "greeted" by 677—a very impressive sight. Additional restoration by the museum team will be required to seal aircraft components from the elements.

To the best of the museum's knowledge, there are seventeen B-52D Models remaining worldwide. 677 has had an extraordinary history, and the museum is thankful to be able to tell her story for years to come.

The Sopwith Camel story appeared in the September 2021 issue of *Aviation History* magazine published by Historynet.com; the B-52 story first appeared as "Combat Veteran Buff" in *Aviation History*, Vol. 30, No. 5, May 2020. Various edits have been made to the original articles.

FOUR

Innovation in Detroit and Dearborn

Tri-Motor at The Henry Ford Museum—courtesy of the author.

Detroit and Dearborn were innovation hotbeds in the 1920s. Perhaps the best remembered innovation of the era was Ford Motor's Tri-Motor—one of the most important aircraft in aviation history—which helped launch many related air travel advances.

Ford Motor's involvement goes back to the earliest known flight in Detroit, which took place in 1909. The aircraft used was modeled on the Bleriot XI, the first heavier-than-air aircraft to cross the English

Channel. The local aircraft was suggested by Ford Motor employee Charles Van Auken and used a Model T engine.

Ford Motor's other early interests included building Liberty airplane engines, which were used in World War I aircraft such as the De Havilland DH-4. Ford Motor used new techniques to expedite cylinder production for these engines.

Edsel Ford became president of Ford Motor in 1919. Both Henry and Edsel Ford were very interested in new aviation technologies, which must have seemed like an extension of the automotive world, and the potential for providing mass transportation for people. The Fords developed the concept of the Ford Reliability Air Tours, where aircraft competed against each other for a trophy, which began in 1925.

Another key aviation personality was William "Bill" Stout. Stout was a descendant of David Bushnell, who built a primitive submarine known as "The Turtle" during the American Revolution. An Illinois native, Stout came to the Detroit area, worked for several automotive businesses, and then formed Stout Engineering Laboratories in 1919.

Stout Engineering worked on various aircraft design projects with the Navy's support. The Navy withdrew its funding after one of these projects crashed, leading to the company's focus on commercial aviation and the creation of a new enterprise—Stout Metal Airplane Company.

To obtain needed financing, Stout sent letters to prominent business people in and out of the auto industry in 1922. He ultimately asked for $1,000 from each potential investor with his only promise being they would *not* be paid back; the selling point was a ground floor opportunity for the future. The fundraising campaign was a huge success. Investors included industrial magnates such as Walter Chrysler, the Fisher brothers, Horace Dodge, and Ransom Olds.

Stout was contacted by Ford Motor's chief engineer William Mayo, who arranged a meeting with Henry and Edsel Ford. Both men contributed to the venture, providing added credibility to Stout's work.

One of Stout's earliest airplanes was the 2-AT, a single-engine monoplane holding up to eight passengers and crew. The "AT" stood for Air Transport and was first test flown in March 1924. In a play on words, this aircraft was named "Maiden Detroit."

The second 2-AT manufactured ("Maiden Dearborn") flew in April 1925 on the Ford Air Transport Service's first flight. Henry Ford created this venture for mail and freight service between different Ford Motor plants; it was not a passenger airline. The initial flight was from Dearborn to Bryan, Ohio, then to Chicago's Maywood Field; it carried over 1,000 pounds of freight. On arrival in Chicago the 2-AT was reloaded and flown back to Dearborn. In February 1926, Ford Air Transport Service was the first contractor carrying airmail for the U.S. Post Office.

The 2-AT's success led to Stout persuading Henry and Edsel Ford to finance an airport and a factory for the Metal Airplane Company in Dearborn. The factory was built on Ford property and began operations in October 1924.

In July 1925, Henry Ford purchased all the stock and assets of the Metal Airplane Company, while retaining Stout and the employees. The business was renamed "Stout Metal Aircraft—A Division of Ford Motor Company." Henry Ford was quoted in the *New York Post* in August 1925: "What the Ford Motor Company means to do is to prove whether commercial flying can be done safely and profitably." Ford Motor then made its first ever aircraft sale of a 2-AT bought by the John Wanamaker department store in New York City. The aircraft was displayed in the store's lobby.

At this point, the story goes down two different, but overlapping paths: one dealing with U.S. passenger airline development, and the second being development of one of the best-known aircraft in aviation history—the Ford Tri-Motor.

Bill Stout, in addition to his aircraft manufacturing responsibilities, founded Stout Airline Service. SAS offered the first regularly scheduled passenger airline in the U.S. flying a Dearborn–Grand Rapids route. Service began in July 1926 with Stout working with Grand Rapids officials to improve their airport, such as removing tree stumps from the runways.

Henry Ford did not allow Ford Field to be operated on Sundays (Henry's wife Clara Ford disapproved of commercial activity on the Sabbath), so SAS flights were advertised as "Daily Except Sundays." As this was a competitive factor, SAS began using a small Romulus airfield—Wayne County Airport—for Sunday travel. This airport later became Detroit Metropolitan Wayne County Airport.

Given Stout's nature as an innovator, it is no surprise SAS pioneered many air travel enhancements. Innovations included pilots wearing uniforms; the first passenger terminal; the first hotel ticket center (at the Book-Cadillac Hotel in Detroit); ticket refunds if cancellations were made two hours before flight; and the first use of aerial couriers (stewards). Airfare included free bus transportation to airports in Detroit, Chicago, and Cleveland and a thirty-pound luggage allowance.

Stout employee Stanley Knauss developed Flight Report sheets for controlling operations, piloting, weather reports, and maintenance checks—adding process discipline for increased safety. Ford Motor built the Dearborn Inn across the street from the Ford Airport, believed to be the second U.S. hotel built to accommodate air travelers.

SAS was purchased in 1929 by National Air Transport, which then merged with Boeing's United Aircraft and Transport Corporation in 1930, becoming United Airlines. United president Fredric Rentschler stated: "We didn't buy airplanes, we bought (Stout's) company that has developed the idea of running an airline as a commercial organization."

Stout continued working on aircraft development with the Metal Airplane Division (he must have had long workweeks). After the 2-AT, the next generation of Stout-designed aircraft was the 3-AT, built in 1925—envisioned as being bigger and better than its 2-AT predecessor.

However, the first 3-AT flights had performance problems; the pilot cut the flight short and told Henry Ford "forget this plane." While problems were understandable as aeronautical engineering was in its infancy, Henry Ford was very upset. The press/public were invited to see the initial flight of the 3-AT, and Ford did not appreciate this public embarrassment.

Stout was relieved of aircraft design duties after the 3-AT episode but remained as an employee. The new lead aircraft designer was Harold Hicks, and he had a staff engineer named James McDonnell. Later in life, McDonnell formed McDonnell Aircraft, producing several iconic aircraft such as the F-4 Phantom.

In January 1926, fate intervened with a fire destroying the 3-AT as well as its storage hangar. This loss was a blessing in disguise, however as a new hangar was built and work began on a significantly improved design—the 4-AT Ford Tri-Motor, which is instantly recognizable and some of which are still flying today.

Hicks and his team moved quickly. The 4-AT's first test flight was made by Ford Motor's chief pilot R.W. Schroeder in June 1926. The 4-AT was a significant improvement over the 3-AT, and initial test flights went exceptionally well. The aircraft was over 49 feet long with a 74-foot wingspan. At the time, it was the largest commercial airplane ever built in the U.S. Cruising speed was 90 miles per hour with three Wright J-4 engines, each producing 200 horsepower.

Ford Motor built the aircraft to be reliable and economical to service. The control cables were on the fuselage's exterior for easy access. As a safety feature, the aircraft was designed to be able to fly on less than three engines. A few automotive parts were recycled from the Model T on the Tri-Motor, such as the bar brake lever, located between the pilot and co-pilot's seats.

Early Tri-Motors had eleven wicker seats, no heater, and were very loud. Cotton was offered to passengers as soundproofing, although it was likely ineffective. Sandwiches were served during flights, and a small lavatory was on board. While primitive by today's standards, Tri-Motors were a huge advancement from other aircraft of the era.

There were many manufacturing innovations associated with these aircraft. A 1928 advertisement in *Aviation* read "Ford airplanes now built by continuous production methods." Tri-Motors were constructed with a new aluminum alloy, Alclad, which was lightweight and strong and avoided the corrosion with the duralumin alloy that had previously been used.

Improvements were steady: the 5-AT, introduced in June 1928, was equipped with new, more powerful Pratt & Whitney Wasp engines. Cruising speed increased to 112 mph and capacity was now over 3,700 pounds of passengers or freight. These improvements allowed Ford Motor to increase the 5-AT's sales price to $65,000— up from $50,000.

By 1930, the company held or had applied for thirty-five aviation-related patents generated by the Tri-Motors.

Aviation-related technologies also evolved as air travel expanded. The new Sperry Beacon provided lighting near airports for night or bad weather flying. These lights, which could be seen 100 miles away, were a huge help to pilots. New radio beacons provided navigational assistance and additional support for night and bad weather travel. Ford Motor had patented the radio beacon but did not charge royalties or fees to other airlines, promoting safe air travel for all.

The Ford Airport in Dearborn covered over 700 acres of land; ultimately, 260 acres on the field's north side were set aside for the Edison Institute, which became the Henry Ford Museum and Greenfield Village. The earliest Tri-Motors had a tail skid instead of a rear wheel, which tore up grass fields. Concrete was needed for an all-weather landing surface and tires were better suited for concrete. Henry Ford promptly issued orders to cover the field with concrete.

Ford Motor seemed to have a limitless future in aviation, but the combination of several factors led Ford Motor to return to its primary automotive business. Harry Brooks, a personal friend of Henry Ford, had died in a crash of a smaller Ford "Flivver" aircraft. Brooks's death apparently had a big impact on Henry Ford. Ultimately, the economics of manufacturing and selling aircraft changed, as the Depression reduced aircraft sales. Competitors such as Boeing and Douglas were developing more innovative aircraft designs and Tri-Motors were becoming obsolete, and Ford Motor did not wish to spend the money necessary for new designs.

The last Tri-Motor manufactured was sold to Pan American Airways in 1932. At that time, air division employees were either transferred to automotive operations or laid off. The airport site eventually became a Ford Motor vehicle test track.

Even though aviation technology moved on, Tri-Motors continued appearing in aviation history, far-removed from U.S. passenger flights. A Tri-Motor was flown over the South Pole in 1929; Edsel Ford contributed $100,000 to the effort and obtained an additional $100,000 from J.D. Rockefeller. The aircraft was a specially modified 4-AT, which was transported by boat to the "Little America" base in Antarctica. That flight was crewed by Richard Byrd, pilot Bernt Balchen, radio operator Harold June, and map photographer A.C. McKinley.

From their base, the flight was about ten hours, one-way, and reached the South Pole at 1:15 a.m. local time. The team carried food provisions for several days in case they were forced down, but these were thrown overboard to clear a high mountain pass. Reaching their destination was determined by a compass reading, and three American flags were dropped on the site. The flags were in honor of Floyd Bennett, who along with Byrd made the first flight over the North Pole (it is uncertain if that flight actually reached the North Pole) and Antarctica explorers Roald Amundsen and Robert Scott.

The Tri-Motor was successfully flown back to Little America, but was left behind when the team sailed home. Byrd returned in 1933, finding the Tri-Motor covered in ice. Byrd and his team chipped off ice, cleaned the carburetors, replaced the battery, and added fresh gas. Incredibly, the engines started and the Tri-Motor flew.

Tri-Motors continued to be used for years with some unique stories, which include flying:

- to small, remote communities in Central and South America, as Tri-Motors could use very short airfields for landings and takeoffs.
- smokejumpers to remote areas of the western U.S. to fight fires.
- then-Governor Franklin Roosevelt to Chicago to accept the Democratic Party's presidential nomination, becoming the first presidential candidate to fly.
- the first baseball team to a game—the Cincinnati Reds traveled to Chicago to play the Cubs—several players did not want to fly and took the train.
- personnel out of Bataan in the early days of World War II, until this aircraft was destroyed on the ground by a Japanese attack.
- passengers from Port Clinton to islands in the Put-In-Bay area on Ohio's Island Airways.

Michigan has three of these aircraft: Dearborn's Henry Ford Museum has the Tri-Motor used on the Antarctica mission; Portage's Air Zoo Aerospace & Science Museum has a Tri-Motor that was used for smoke jumping by the U.S. Forest Service (The aircraft was rebuilt, flown for several years, and is now a static display); and Belleville's Yankee Air Museum acquired a flyable Tri-Motor previously flown by Ohio's Island Airways. Visitors to any of these facilities can see close up one of the most important aircraft designs in aviation history.

FIVE

———————————◯———————————

Talbert "Ted" Abrams—
Father of Aerial Photography

Ted Abrams—courtesy of the Barbara J. Brown Collection, Archives of Michigan.

He's called the "father of aerial photography," yet Talbert "Ted" Abrams's role as an aerial photographer is only a small part of his impressive legacy in Michigan, where he was a leader in aviation, technology, business, and philanthropy.

Born in 1895, Abrams grew up on a farm in Tekonsha, Michigan—
about thirty miles southeast of Battle Creek. Abrams was the youngest
of William Abrams and Sarah Bruner's four children. Family lore
suggests his father wanted his son to carry on the farm, but it was not to
be. When he was eight years old, Talbert began developing his lifelong
passion for aviation when he heard his father exclaim: "The Wright Boys
had flown!" A 1941 *Detroit Free Press* article reported a different slant—as
a boy, Abrams delivered pulp fiction novels with aviation themes, piqu-
ing his interest.

Whatever the story, in the pre-World War 1 years, young Abrams
began working at aviation companies in Detroit, Ohio, and New York.
While working in non-glamorous jobs such as grinding valves at a
Glen Curtiss (an early U.S. aviation pioneer) factory in Buffalo—the
valve-grinding job helped pay the $1.50/minute cost of flying lessons.

After the U.S. entered World War I in 1917, Abrams joined an
aviation unit in the Marine Corps and went on his first solo flight a year
later. He was stationed in Florida, then was assigned to patrol duty in the
Caribbean, taking aerial photos over Cuba, Haiti, and the Dominican
Republic. He took photos from the cockpit using the limited technology
of the day, the experience likely planting the seed that many improvements were needed.

When he returned to the civilian world in 1919, Abrams became an
airmail pilot—an extremely dangerous endeavor given the primitive
aircraft, communications, and navigation equipment available. Another
early venture was a flying barnstorming show—Abrams noted he would
do almost anything "to buy coffee and donuts." Archival records show
an advertisement of an Abrams parachute jump over Eaton Rapids from
3,000 feet; family members believe Abrams and his wife Leota may have
been wing-walkers in those early shows.

Besides the considerable risk, Abrams likely assumed that barnstorming was not the way to provide a comfortable lifestyle. He also
found that people were more interested in photographs taken from the
air than actually going on an airplane ride, so another element of what
became Abrams's career path fell into place. One story had it that a local

newspaper wanted an aerial shot of a racetrack; Abrams borrowed a camera, took off, and took the photo for a $10 fee.

The aviation industry of the 1920s was uncharted territory—risky, expensive, and financially uncertain. This is when Abrams's entrepreneurial spirit kicked in, combining his flying skills and innovative mind with sharp business acumen.

In 1922, Abrams founded the ABC (Always Be Careful) Airline in Lansing, which was renamed Abrams Aerial Survey Corporation (AASC) a year later. Business was slow at first in the new industry of aerial surveying.

It was not long, however, before government agencies and businesses recognized the intrinsic value of aerial photography. In September 1925, AASC provided an early aerial survey for the Michigan State Highway Department. Using Abrams-developed aerial cameras, the survey photographed the route for a major north-south road in Michigan. This route later became U.S. 27—one the first highways built using aerial photographs. Abrams obtained Federation Aeronautique International Pilot License No. 282—issued in 1926 and signed by Orville Wright—the Federation was the pilot-licensing organization of the times.

Abrams soon expanded the company by purchasing new airplanes and cameras, hiring employees, and finding customers for aerial maps of flood control areas, highways, power lines, and other land-use purposes. Additionally, he revolutionized the science of photogrammetry, which creates precise measurements from recording, measuring, and interpreting photographic images.

The Michigan Archives in Lansing have thousands of photographs and negatives with AASC's work, covering a wide range of locations throughout Michigan. A 1932–1956 collection includes landmarks such as Detroit's Ambassador Bridge, Sault Ste Marie's Soo Locks, Mackinaw Island, and Isle Royale. The Isle Royale work involved flying at an altitude of over 12,000 feet and taking over 200 photos. These shots were compiled into a 30' x 6' wall map, later reduced to scale by the United States Geological Survey. Abrams's flights over Isle Royale included images of moose, other wildlife, and several previously unmapped lakes on the island.

AASC's customer base was varied and included state and federal agencies, counties, municipalities, and private companies. A 1934 advertising pamphlet noted the Public Works Administration, Civilian Conservation Corp, and the Tennessee Valley Authority among its customers.

Abrams's business acumen translated science and technology into profits, funding future research. Abrams noted "it was cheaper to incorporate and limit our liability than it was to buy insurance." In one calculation, he determined that in a four-hour flight, an extra 10 miles an hour in air speed could increase gross income by $200 a day—a significant sum during the Depression. Survey costs ranged between $0.01 and $0.10 an acre in 1934.

In addition to his entrepreneurial skills, Abrams was an inventor. For example, he filed a patent application in January 1930 for an "air view contour finder," which used several lenses and reflectors designed to highlight the contours of land areas (the patent was granted in 1932). Contour finders were key in converting photographs into three-dimensional images, providing tremendous utility for both military and civilian purposes. Abrams's vision was to make the device low-cost and easy to produce and to operate. These technological advancements led to starting Lansing-based Abrams Instruments, which opened in 1938.

The first aircraft Abrams used for photogrammetry was a Standard J-1, a two seat World War I era aircraft. The J-1 had a hole cut in the fuselage floor for taking photos—clearly a process in its infancy. Other conventional aircraft, used subsequent to the J-1, had front-mounted engines (limiting visibility), were loud (making cockpit communication difficult), tended to leak oil (which could cover up a camera lens), and vibrated (reducing photo quality).

The limits of these aircraft led Ted to launching Abrams Aircraft in 1937 from which a one-of-a-kind "Explorer" aircraft was designed. The Explorer, built at the Page Buggy Company in Marshall, Michigan, was designed specifically for reconnaissance purposes, with a rear engine and a very large plexiglass nose for increased visibility. The U.S. military, however, found the Explorer too slow for military combat operations and used combat aircraft, adapted to reconnaissance work, for these missions. As a result, the original Abrams Explorer was phased out in 1948 and is now at a Smithsonian storage facility in Maryland.

Ever the Renaissance man, Abrams also taught classes in surveying and photogrammetry at Michigan State College (now Michigan State University) in East Lansing, beginning in 1926. In 1944, Abrams wrote and published a book, *Essentials of Aerial Surveying and Photo Interpretation*. His text was used by Marine surveyors and photo interpreters at the Abrams School of Aerial Surveying and Photo Interpretation during World War II.

Abrams's impact during World War II was very significant, both in Michigan and worldwide. U.S. and allied armed forces made significant use of aerial reconnaissance, using techniques and knowledge developed by Abrams. These innovations directly contributed to the Allied victory. As U.S. Admiral Richmond K. Turner acknowledged: "Photographic reconnaissance has been our main source of intelligence in the Pacific. Its importance cannot be overemphasized."

In addition to the air contour finder, Abrams obtained patents for devices such as a 16mm combat gun camera, anti-fogging devices for gun sights, and a radar camera—all highly beneficial to the Allied war effort.

Michigan likewise reaped enormous benefits from Abrams's work. His aerial photography spurred efficiencies in roadbuilding, accurate road mapping, and commercial and residential construction. Abrams stated in a 1939 *Military Engineering* article that less than 5 percent of the land area worldwide had been effectively mapped—an estimated 56 million square miles total. Abrams ended up surveying a good chunk of it. Abrams and his companies mapped over 1,700 U.S. cities, 500 counties, and worked on over 1,000 international projects. Decades later, these communities continue to benefit from his work. He traveled extensively —eight times around the world—becoming Pan American Airlines' frequent flier #1.

Abrams eventually became a philanthropist. He donated a Beechcraft AT-11 Kansan aircraft, previously used for aerial photography, to the National Museum of the United States Air Force in Dayton, Ohio, where it is on display. He funded the purchase of the land and a monument at Meridian State Park (Ingham/Jackson County, Michigan) marking the surveying spot for measuring Michigan townships and parts of Ohio. Through engineering associations, he sponsored academic scholarships.

Abrams crossed paths with some of Michigan's most renowned leaders in aviation. One of AASC's chief pilots was Ypsilanti resident Albert Kettles, who served in this role from the late 1940s until his 1966 retirement. Kettles had his own prominent career in aviation and is profiled in chapter 13.

There was much more to Ted Abrams than airplanes, instruments, and photographs. Wayland Mayo, AASC's Chief Photographer for seven years in the mid-60s, described Abrams as "distinguished, impressive, and charismatic," and added "the world is a better place because of him." Abrams's management team was described as "very meticulous, insisting on nothing less than absolute perfection in the production of precision maps." This dedication to excellence was established at the top by Ted Abrams.

A very partial list of honors received by Abrams includes:

Mount Abrams in Antarctica was named in his honor based on his support of the Ronne Antarctic Research Expedition. Following the original 1947–48 Ronne expedition, Abrams himself made two trips to the South Pole in Operation Deep Freeze (1960s) and to the North Pole as part of Operation Frigid (1948). The Air Force led both of these missions.

Abrams has been inducted into the Michigan Transportation Hall of Fame and was the first honorary member in the Michigan Society of Registered Land Surveyors. He received three honorary degrees from Western Michigan University in Kalamazoo, Michigan State University, and the Michigan College of Mining and Technology (now Michigan Technological University) in Houghton.

An essential part of the Ted Abrams story is his wife, Leota Pearl Fry, who he married in 1923. Leota was involved in social work and was, in the language of her day, an *aviatrix*, being the first woman to obtain her pilot's license at Lansing's Capital City airport in 1930. She flew in the 1931 Michigan Air Race and several Michigan Air Tours. She was an astute businesswoman, serving on the board of directors of Ted's companies, and was a force to be reckoned with—described as "assertive" and as "Ted's crutch" in a family history. Ted was the public face of the various Abrams enterprises, but there is little doubt that Leota was his lifelong partner in every sense of the word.

In the early 1960s, Ted and Leota founded the Abrams Foundation. Foundation management was assumed by their niece Barbara Burt Brown in 1985. Ms. Brown led the Foundation for twenty-six years until her death in 2011. It is now led by Abrams's grand-niece Kyle Abbott. The Foundation provided funding for Michigan State University's Abrams Planetarium, as well as science, education, and human services projects. It also underwrites the Abrams Genealogy Collection at the State of Michigan Archives.

In 1950, Ted and his wife Leota were considering options for a new home in the Lansing area. While on a flight over the Atlantic Ocean, the couple saw the shadow of their airplane on a rainbow-hued cloud. Inspiration hit—they decided to design their house in the shape of an airplane. This Lansing home does not have an attic or basement; the "ends" of the house are rounded to symbolize aircraft wingtips and a curved front window is made of plexiglass. A wooden propeller was mounted on an interior wall of the home.

Family members today describe visits to the airplane house as formal occasions; Ted and Leota could be somewhat intimidating. But there was a playful side to Ted Abrams as well, as when he impishly smiled to one of his visiting grand-nieces or nephews, saying "One day, I'm going to take you to the moon." It seems entirely possible Abrams was reminiscing about his youth, delivering those pulp detective works in rural Michigan.

The companies Abrams founded were eventually sold; the family is no longer involved in their operation. Leota passed away in 1978; Ted died in 1990. Their very considerable talents and generosity live on in

Michigan and throughout the world, and will do so for many years to come.

This chapter first appeared as "Talbert Abrams, The Father of Aerial Photography" in *Chronicle,* a magazine published by the Historical Society of Michigan, Vol. 43, No. 2, Summer 2020 www.hsmichigan. org. Various edits have been made to the original article.

SIX

Suzanne Parish and the Kalamazoo Air Zoo

Suzanne Parish as a WASP—courtesy of the Air Zoo Aerospace and Science Museum.

Suzanne DeLano Parish was a Renaissance woman: a high-ly-skilled aviatrix, equestrian, philanthropist, and actress as well as co-founding one of the country's leading aviation museums.

Her family tree is equally impressive. Parish's grandfather, Dr. William E. Upjohn was founder of the Upjohn Pharmaceutical Company. Parish's mother, Dorothy DeLano, was related distantly to Presidents Ulysses S. Grant and Franklin Delano Roosevelt.

Parish was born in November 1922 in New York City, though she lived in Europe until age seven. In 1929, her family settled in Kalamazoo where she started first grade on the grounds of what is now Western Michigan University (WMU). Always precocious, young Suzanne had a few pet mice and from time to time would put the mice in the teacher's desk—getting the expected gasp when the teacher opened the drawer. This spiritedness was indicative of Parish doing things on her own terms—a trait that defined her entire life.

Throughout her youth, Parish had a passion for horseback riding and was a highly skilled equestrian. An undated headline in the *Kalamazoo Gazette* newspaper, "Crowd Sees Sue DeLano Win Horse Show Honors," highlighted her talents, which inadvertently led her to her true-life passion—flying.

Once she graduated from high school, she attended Sarah Lawrence college in Bronxville, New York, and then joined the Kalamazoo chapter of the United Service Organizations in 1942. One of her tasks was distributing food and treats to troops travelling through the area on trains.

In 1942, after injuring her ankle and heel from falling off a horse, her mom suggested she follow in the footsteps of her cousin, Dr. Richard Light: "Your cousin Dick flies and likes it. Why don't you take a few flying lessons until you can ride again?" Parish listened to her mom's counsel and took to the skies.

At an unpaved Austin Lake, Michigan, airstrip, Light took her up in a small, single-engine aircraft. That first ride did it—Suzanne Parish was forever hooked on aviation.

There were few women pilots when Parish began flying. She got lost on her first solo flight from Austin Lake, and because she was low on gas, landed on a farmer's field. She called her instructor, Irving Woodhams, from the farmer's home. Woodhams had another pilot fly him to the farm and then provided Parish fuel, navigation tips, and stern silence on the return flight until he said at the end, "I guess you can land now." A lesson learned from her mentor Woodhams, who would later become the first pilot to fly solo at Lindbergh Field (site of the future Kalamazoo/Battle Creek International Airport).

She continued flying after the DeLano family moved to Arizona in 1943. With World War II gas rationing limits, Parish chose to ride her horse fourteen miles round trip to a very small, one landing strip airport—now Phoenix Sky Harbor International Airport—for flying lessons. The lessons were successful and Parish received her pilots license by April that same year.

Shortly thereafter, she applied to join the Women Air Service Pilots (WASP). Because Parish didn't meet the twenty-one-years-old minimum age requirement, the WASPs declined her application until she became of age in 1944, when Parish graduated with the class 44-W-6 at Avenger airfield in Sweetwater, Texas.

Post-graduation, Parish and another WASP reported to the Advanced Instrument School at Bryan Army Air base in Texas. The base commander told the new students: "I didn't send for you...I know that being women you can't pass this course."

How wrong he was! Parish and her fellow WASPs passed, turning around the commander's previous low opinion of female pilots. From that time forward, their value was acknowledged as they became indispensable at the Bryan Army Air base. At the final WASP class graduation in December 1944, General Henry H. Arnold noted: "We of the Army Air Force are proud of you; we will never forget our debt to you." A praise clearly intended for all WASPs, including Sue Parish.

As World War II was winding down, Parish wrote to a number of commercial airlines, looking for flying work. All of them sent rejection letters, which often noted her flying skills and then stated female pilots were not in their hiring plans. For example, American Airlines' December 1944 rejection letter contained the following: "While we sincerely appreciate your flying experience and background, we are sorry to advise that we are unable to consider women in a flight capacity other than stewardess."

Undeterred, Parish contacted her uncle Donald Gilmore, chairman of Upjohn Pharmaceuticals, for a corporate pilot position. No luck—not even family ties could overcome the fact that commercial aviation simply was not ready for female pilots.

For several years after World War II, she found work as a driver for the American Red Cross, which included transporting amputees at Fort Custer in Battle Creek to the Kellogg Manor House rehabilitation center at Gull Lake, Michigan.

Life moved on without flying. She married Preston (Pete) Parish in 1948, who was born in Chicago in 1919. Pete was a Marine war hero in World War II, receiving the Bronze Star and other citations for actions in battle on Peleliu and Guadalcanal. He began receiving Naval aviation training, but the war ended before he received his wings (which the Navy finally awarded in 1984). Pete Parish had a civilian pilots license and a distinguished career in business and aviation.

The Parishes had five children in six years, with Sue choosing to be a stay-at-home mom. In 1959, Pete bought a half interest in a Beechcraft aircraft. This was great news, as Sue Parish now had an opportunity to resume flying again.

The Air Zoo

By the 1970s, the Parishes had a small collection of airplanes and got to thinking: *In addition to preserving these aircraft, why not display them to the public as well?* Local businessman Gunther Balz, owner of a Grumman F8F Bearcat (which came online but did not see combat at the end of World War II), agreed and offered to donate his aircraft to the Parishes if they opened a museum.

Thus, the Kalamazoo Air History Museum was founded in 1977; the original museum was in a building used by a local Piper aircraft distributor and Fixed Base Operator. The museum opened to the public in November 1979 with a fleet of nine aircraft in a 17,500-square-foot facility. An original vision for the museum was to house a collection of World War II flyable aircraft—and of the original nine, six were air-worthy. In addition to Balz's F8F, other World War II classics included a Grumman F4F Wildcat, a Curtiss P-40 Warhawk, and a Chance-Vought F4U Corsair.

As one would expect, a start-up aviation museum required much work from many people. The first employee was Bob Ellis, who was hired as General Manager and ultimately became the Air Zoo's President and CEO. Bob's brother John Ellis, among many other activities, was the Air Zoo's Chief Pilot. John had been a Naval aviator and helped establish safety and related requirements for Air Zoo aircraft—essential work, given the risks of flying high performance aircraft at low altitudes.

The museum was renamed the Air Zoo Aerospace and Science Museum, with the "Zoo" coming from the collection's animal-named aircraft, such as the Bearcat and Wildcat. The Air Zoo is now one of Michigan's leading tourist attractions, has completed several expansions, and now includes the Michigan Space and Science Center, which had been in Jackson. With over 200,000 square feet of display and office space, guests will find aircraft, exhibits, artifacts, and educational programming for visitors of all ages.

Both Parishes were long-time board members participating in strategic planning and other leadership tasks. Bill Painter, one of the Air Zoo's first volunteers, noted Sue's high standards and that she was not bashful about providing direction to the staff.

Visitors to the Air Zoo will immediately notice a pink Curtiss P-40 Warhawk suspended from the lobby's ceiling. This 1944-built aircraft, which did not see combat in World War II, is now painted in a pink-hued "Desert tan" camouflage. Various civilians owned the aircraft after the war before Parish acquired it. To keep it historically authentic, Parish consulted with the Smithsonian on the color scheme where she learned the paint would often fade in the harsh African sun to a pink tinge.

It took three years of restoration to make the P-40 flyable. Parish trained in a North American AT-6, then along with Frank Sanders, a pilot who led the restoration effort, and flew the aircraft to Kalamazoo from California. Parish also flew the P-40 to various air shows around the country, where she often completed aerial acrobatics and where the men flying vintage aircraft might have been taken aback seeing Parish climbing out of the cockpit after landing—women warbird pilots were few and far between.

Parish and the P-40 participated in a 1983 flyover of Washington D.C. commemorating the movie *The Right Stuff*, a dramatized account of the space program's early days. One of America's most famous pilots, Chuck Yeager, who was profiled in the movie, flew a North American P-51 Mustang for this event. The P-40 was retired from flying in 1993 and was moved to its current location ten years later.

Parish and the Air Zoo participated in several unconventional projects in addition to the lobby display of the P-40. She, along with others from the Air Zoo team, traveled to Greenland in 1989 to evaluate salvaging a Boeing B-29 that had crash-landed after World War II. The project turned out to be very complex and was taken over by another group. Unfortunately, this B-29 was later destroyed in a fire, and the remnants remain in Greenland.

Sue Parish received many honors in her lifetime. In 1984, all of the WASPs were awarded the World War II Victory Medal. Sue Parish was the first woman honored in the Experimental Aircraft Association Hall of Fame's "Warbirds" category in October 1997. She retired from flying in March 1999 at age seventy-six, with over 8,000 air hours in a wide range of military and civilian aircraft types. In July 2009, Parish and the other surviving WASPs received the Congressional Gold Medal for their World War II service, and she was inducted into WMU's College of Aviation Hall of Honor in 2010.

Renaissance Woman

Suzanne Parish had a wide range of interests in addition to the Air Zoo. She was always a generous benefactor to charities, carrying on the tradition of the Upjohn family (her grandfather Dr. William Upjohn was named "Person of the Century" by the *Kalamazoo Gazette* newspaper for his philanthropic support in 2000). Parish's philanthropy included the 1984 establishment of the Suzanne Upjohn Delano Parish Foundation, awarding grants to numerous Michigan non-profit organizations.

In 1974, the Parishes established a small charter airline called SP/Air. One of SP/Air's most famous passengers was comedian Bob Hope who chartered a flight from Kalamazoo to Chicago. Hope was not aware that a woman would be the pilot until Pete Parish told him just before boarding. Taken aback, Hope said, "You're kidding…look what the lady libbers are doing to us now!" Parish also participated in the "Angel Wings" program, which transports patients needing specialized assistance to hospitals such as the Mayo Clinic.

Sue was always generous with her aircraft. For example, she loaned her Cessna 425 Conquest twin-engine propeller aircraft to WMU in 2004 and provided substantial financial support to keep it flying. Parish always encouraged students, particularly young women, to consider aviation careers.

Theater was another talent of this multifaceted woman. Her acting career began after World War II in a production of *Morning at Seven*, when acting was put on hold as family responsibilities took precedence. In 1982, Parish was asked to reprise her role of Cora in *Morning at Seven*; she then acted in other productions such as *Arsenic and Old Lace,* where a local review said "her mannerisms and carriage were perfect for the part." Much as she loved being on stage (the Suzanne D. Parish Theater in Kalamazoo is named after her), flying always came first—she once missed a rehearsal to fly the P-40 to a Minnesota air show.

Later in life she also studied photography, travelling to locations all over the world, published a cookbook of family recipes and an autobiography "Sue Parish Memoirs" in 2012. In her memoir, Sue Parish noted her number one goal in her life was to be a good mother. And, whatever the task at hand—family, business, philanthropy—she wanted to excel. Bob Ellis described Parish as someone who had "never known the meaning of the word 'no.'"

Her Legacy

The Air Zoo continues to move forward, acquiring a Lockheed F-117 Nighthawk in 2020. This stealth attack fighter was developed at the "Skunk Works," Lockheed's research and development group that had developed many cutting-edge aircraft. In another Michigan connection, the guiding force behind the Skunk Works, Clarence "Kelly" Johnson, was born in Ishpeming and attended the University of Michigan.

Suzanne Parish's legacy is tremendous. Her accomplishments as a WASP, museum cofounder, and mother of five were remarkable by any standard. One of her sons, Will Parish, describes his mother's attributes best: She had a "determination to learn, presence of mind under pressure, unsurpassed pilot skills, and most importantly, perseverance." Sue Parish passed away in 2010.

This chapter first appeared as "From Aviator to the Air Zoo, The Life of Suzanne Parish" in *Michigan History,* a magazine published by the Historical Society of Michigan, Vol. 104, No. 5, September/ October 2020 www.hsmichigan.org. Various edits have been made to the original article.

SEVEN

○

Michigan's Gliders go to War

"The Fighting Falcon" at the Air Zoo—courtesy of the author.

Michigan's World War II glider production concluded in 1945, but what remains today is a compelling story of hard work, ingenuity, and some patriotic school kids who did their part to defeat the Axis.

Fleets of engineless gliders were towed to a combat area by powered aircraft, cut loose, and then flown by pilots to landing areas behind enemy lines. Gliders were a key part of many Word War II campaigns including the invasion of Sicily, the D-Day landings in Normandy, the air invasion of Northern Europe, and the campaign to liberate Burma from the Japanese., The goal of Waco glider formattions was delivering concentrated masses of troops, ammunition, and other military equipment directly to critical target areas, literally bringing the troops to the enemy's doorstep. Gliders delivered critical medics and supplies to Bastogne during December 1944's Battle of the Bulge.

Glider crews may not have had the cachet of fighter pilots, but it was a very high-risk occupation. As there was no engine, glider pilots had no second chance to retry landings once the tow rope was released. Glider construction resulted in a very loud aircraft—war correspondent Walter Cronkite, who flew on a September 1944 mission, commented "it was like being inside the drum at a Grateful Dead concert."

Pilots surviving the landing (often a controlled crash in the dark) might be miles behind enemy lines and would join forces with his infantrymen passengers. Lt. General James Gavin, commander of the 82nd Airborne during World War II, remarked: "Having to land a glider in combat for the first time is a chastening experience; it gives a man religion."

CG-4As were the primary U.S. glider during the war and were designed by Weaver Aircraft Company (Waco) in Troy, Ohio. CG-4As could carry fifteen troops, including the pilot and co-pilot, and the nose could be raised to load and unload cargo. Almost 14,000 CG-4As were produced in two plants in Michigan: The Iron Mountain Ford Motor Company plant in Kingsford (adjacent to Iron Mountain) and Gibson Refrigerator in Greenville.

Wherever manufactured, CG-4As were complex with more than 70,000 parts and 2,500 pages of underlying blueprints. Complexity was added from thousands of design modifications requested by the military. The output from both Michigan plants were highly regarded. The 26th Mobile Reclamation and Repair Squadron in England assembled gliders received from the U.S. and noted the Ford and Gibson gliders were easiest to reassemble—a testimony to the production quality at both locations.

The Iron Mountain story began when Henry Ford purchased almost 430,000 acres of land in the area—equivalent to more than half of

Rhode Island. This land was in Iron, Baraga, and Marquette counties. Forest wood logged from the land would be used for Model T automobile production. In August 1920, the Michigan Iron, Land & Lumber Company was organized to manage the Iron Mountain sawmill, body plant, and Ford logging operations in the Upper Peninsula.

Economic hard times caused by the Depression resulted in the layoff of much of the workforce, which once topped 7,000 people. Plant Superintendent Walter Nelson was continually searching for new business opportunities but with little success. Nelson contacted Ford offices shortly after Pearl Harbor, and it was made clear Iron Mountain would likely be shut down if new business was not found.

That changed in March 1942, when the U.S. Government approached Ford about glider production (previous investigation of producing either Higgins boats or a Jeep variant had not worked out). U.S. military planners took note of Germany's successful use of these aircraft in Europe. A glider's wood construction brought Iron Mountain to mind for Ford management, given the abundance of local resources and skilled woodworkers.

Once a contract was in place, Ford wanted to use automotive mass production techniques, consistent with Ford's other aviation ventures— building Tri-Motors in the late 1920s and concurrent production of B-24 Liberators. This was not a simple proposition. Ford completely reworked several buildings at Iron Mountain to accommodate manufacturing needs, using about 400,000 square feet of plant space.

The very first test Ford glider was manufactured in Dearborn and flown in September 1942—and that test flight was observed by Henry and Edsel Ford. The pilot said the glider was "the best he had flown." Production equipment was then sent to Iron Mountain for installation in the plant.

Iron Mountain gliders used mostly Ford-produced components, except for items such as the cockpit's instrumentation. Fuselage frames were subcontracted to companies such as the Lloyd Manufacturing Company in Menominee. The first four Iron Mountain gliders came off the line in December 1942. Once production was underway, completed gliders were either flown/towed from Iron Mountain directly to Army bases, or they were disassembled, sent to Dearborn, reassembled, tested, and then delivered to the Army.

Three shifts, with about 4,500 employees, worked around the clock at the peak of production. The glider's outer "skin" is a representative example of the work—the skin was very thin mahogany plywood, covered by a tough, light-weight cotton fabric. The fabric covering was cut and stitched in a "sewing room" overlooking the assembly line. Two-thirds of this area was occupied by sewing machines; the remainder was used by cutters who knifed out cloth in various sizes. Glider fabric was covered with olive drab weather-resistant coatings, known as "doping."

Successful use of mass production techniques resulted in Iron Mountain having the lowest manufacturing cost ($15,400) of all U.S. glider plants; 4,190 gliders were produced at Iron Mountain, more than any other U.S. plant. Iron Mountain's work resulted in receiving three Army-Navy "E" awards during the war, which were given for production excellence. The end of the war caused operations to shut down in 1945.

Concurrent with Ford's efforts, Gibson Refrigerator produced gliders in Greenville. During the war, Gibson produced materials such as bombs, precision testing gear, anti-aircraft gun parts, as well as gliders. Obtaining the glider contract was not a certainty. Gibson Executive Vice President Louis Hamper had to convince the War Department that production targets could be met. Selling points for Gibson included available space in existing facilities and their large number of experienced wood and metal workers—pre-World War II refrigerators had wood casings.

Once the contract was awarded, Gibson converted production from refrigerators to gliders in six months; the last refrigerator was produced in April 1942. Special provisions were needed in some areas of the plant (which was reconfigured for manufacturing), such as maintaining high humidity conditions to improve the workability of wood parts. The spray dope that tightened and strengthened the fabric also required sufficient ventilation because of the risk of explosion and toxic fumes.

There were no detail parts or any sub-assembly drawings. Gibson personnel, such as nineteen-year-old William Delp (an assistant master mechanic), were highly competent at appliance work, but glider construction was a new world.

Gibson management realized the predicament. President C.G. Taylor of Taylorcraft, an Ohio aircraft manufacturer, was invited to Greenville to review operations. It was clear Gibson needed assistance from experienced aircraft manufacturing personnel. Taylor recommended that Eric Guenther, Taylorcraft's chief aircraft welding engineer, relocate to and work at Greenville.

In early April 1942, Guenther, with his pregnant wife Margaret, interviewed for the job. They checked out the town and a favorable impression of Greenville Hospital helped seal the deal. Guenther became a key employee, setting up a welding school to train the fifty certified welders who were needed. He also provided detail reviews of blueprints, tooling and equipment needs, and plant layout.

Other area businesses were part of the glider team. The nose and pilot's compartment were purchased from Ronan and Kunzl Company in Marshall. Wing assemblies were sub-contracted to a group of area manufacturers known as Grand Rapids Industries.

Gibson's first glider was completed in six months and was flight-tested at the old Grand Rapids airport, about thirty miles away (not the present Gerald R. Ford International Airport). Flight testing presented its own challenges; gliders were first disassembled and crated. Specially designed trucks were needed for hauling the crates over the roadway's curves when travelling to the airport. Flight-tested gliders were returned to Gibson, recrated, and shipped overseas. These very large crates (some were over 20' long) were constructed of high-quality wood; five crates held a complete glider. All major glider sections came apart easily for shipment, and once transported overseas, the wood from their shipping containers was often recycled as base housing.

Total wartime output at Gibson was 1,078 gliders. Gibson's story has one more unique angle—the extraordinary work and support of local school kids. In March 1943, area students began working on a War Bonds sales effort with a goal of selling enough bonds and stamps in the three months before school closed to buy one glider. This was a huge undertaking: a Greenville manufactured glider cost $17,000, and previous bond sales were slow—one week had resulted in $235 of sales. A challenge to increase sales was proposed by the students at an assembly and publicly announced the next day in the *Greenville Daily News*. All local schools participated.

This effort was a huge success—the campaign's first week saw sales of $1,259 of bonds and stamps. Adolf Hitler's April birthday resulted in extra hard work to sell bonds for defeating the Nazis. Students who sold more than $1,000 in bonds included nine-year old Frederick Brace, Jr. and high school students Nina Johnson, Richard Kennedy, Max Larson, Carolyn Packard, Rosellen Raymor, Phyllis Tower, and Nancy Whitelaw.

Seven weeks later, results were announced at another school assembly—the drive had raised more than $72,000, exceeding their goal by 400 percent. In honor of the achievement, Mayor Oscar Rasmussen declared May 19 as Glider Day. A ceremony at the athletic field christened one of the Gibson-built gliders as the "The Flying Falcon," with an additional inscription "Presented by Greenville Schools, Greenville, Michigan."

During the ceremony, Greenville students received the United States Treasury Department's Distinguished Service Award, the first-time school students received this recognition. After the ceremony, the "Flying Falcon" which was the twenty-third Gibson glider produced, was renamed "The Fighting Falcon" as a Gibson executive wanted a "fiercer name." The Falcon was returned to the factory for shipment to England.

Originally, Army Air Force headquarters ordered that the Fighting Falcon be the first of an echelon of fifty-two gliders on D-Day, in recognition of the students' work. As D-Day approached, invasion planners were going to have one of the landing force generals, Brig. General Donald Pratt, land in this glider in a jeep (the nose would be raised and the jeep driven out). However, mission planners decided to use a different glider with a customized nose for this assignment.

So, another Greenville glider was substituted, renamed the "Fighting Falcon" and led the mission. That "substitute" glider was flown by Lt. Col. Michael Murphy, the highest-ranking Army Air Force glider pilot. That glider crashed in Normandy and two passengers, including Pratt, were killed. Murphy was seriously injured and earned a Purple Heart, the Legion of Merit, and other medals for his actions (the glider crash scene in the movie *Saving Private Ryan* is loosely based on Murphy's flight). The original "Fighting Falcon" that was built with funds raised by the school kids landed safely in Normandy.

Several years after the end of the war, area resident Mrs. A.W. Miller wrote a poem about the student's contribution, including these lines:

> The Falcon Flew, as we visioned her.
> The Falcon was bought by our girls and lads,
> But 'twas built by the hands of their mothers and dads.
> Foremost and first, she landed in France
> Giving the enemy nary a chance.

Glider production ceased with war's end, leaving surplus equipment at both factories. Gibson's surplus crated gliders were sometimes sold at auctions for as little as $50 per crate. A December 1945 advertisement solicited interested persons to inspect the gliders and submit bids. Many crates were purchased by farmers who only wanted the wood and would discard the glider contents. Over time, the woods and fields near Greenville and Iron Mountain accumulated scrap parts.

Years later, the Iron Mountain and Greenville glider stories came together at the Air Zoo Aerospace & Science Museum. Darryl Waters, from Haslett, Michigan, was a CG-4A instructor who flew on D-Day. Captured by the Germans, he spent nine months as a POW. Waters began visiting the Air Zoo in the late 1980s, contributing World War II photos and artifacts.

Waters had also found a CG-4A fuselage in the woods near Iron Mountain where it had been used as a shed; his enthusiasm helped convince the Air Zoo to restore this glider. Air Zoo personnel made the trip up north, finding a bare steel framework of the main fuselage section including the nose. It was rusty, bent, and had a six-inch pine tree growing through it.

Searching for parts was an ongoing project. Several rusted fuselages were in Pennsylvania's Pocono Mountains. The owner of a barn in New York collected abandoned aircraft parts—including CG-4A tail surfaces, landing gear, and a complete floor assembly (which would have taken many hours to build from scratch). Outer wing parts were located in northern Michigan; inner panel spars came from Kent City. Additional materials were found in a cave in Colorado where a sub-contractor had stored the parts. The relatively dry conditions preserved them until Air Zoo personnel arrived, decades later.

In addition to the Air Zoo's glider, other aviation museums in Michigan have CG-4As displayed, each with their own unique stories.

Oscoda's Wurtsmith Air Museum has a partially restored CG-4A displayed in a building that was previously an alert hangar for Wurtsmith Air Force Base. The original glider frame was obtained in the 1990s; a ten-year restoration project was led by longtime volunteer William Erb with many components coming from Greenville or the Air Zoo. The glider is named "Peggy Ann" in honor of Erb's late wife. One side of the fuselage was left open so visitors could see the interior seating; it is clear that gliders were not built for comfort.

The Fighting Falcon Military Museum in Greenville has a CG-4A, with the former Gibson team of Eric Guenther and Bill Delp leading the restoration effort long after the war ended. Area residents asked Guenther and Delp to serve as technical advisors to a group of school children called the Young Astronaut Club, who wanted to restore a CG-4A glider for the Flat River Historical Society. A trip to the Air Zoo and a review of their glider whetted the appetite of the Greenville kids to work on this project. The local newspaper provided publicity and the community responded with generous donations; the project took over ten years to complete.

In Iron Mountain, restoration of a CG-4A—and the building of a museum—began with the donation of a deteriorated glider fuselage frame to the Menominee Range Historical Foundation. Olaf and Beatrice Blomquist had purchased the frame for $75 from Ford's Iron Mountain plant after the war. The Blomquist's had sold it to their nephew, Vernon Anderson, for use as a play house and hunting camp. Anderson's family donated the glider in 2005; community support generated enough funds for the restoration and to build the World War II Glider and Military Museum, which opened in July, 2011.

Our Michigan museums commemorate both the manufacturing effort and the bravery of the glider crews during the war. As usual, the generosity of local communities and hardworking volunteers make this possible.

EIGHT

---○---

Neal Loving— An Inspirational Life Story

Neal Vernon Loving said "I have a history of people telling me what I can't do. So far they're all wrong." It wasn't a boast, it was fact. In his lifetime, Loving overcame incredible odds— racial prejudice, physical handicaps, and a childhood of poverty—with limitless determination to become a prominent aviator and lifelong mentor to young people.

Detroit native Loving was born in February 1916, graduating from Detroit's Cass Technical High School and Highland Park Junior College, working long hours to pay for his degree in engineering drafting. Although his father was a trained optometrist (and the first African American to pass Michigan's optometry test in 1925), the senior Loving could not find work because of racial prejudice. The lack of work put a financial strain on the family, resulting in frequent evictions for the family and changes of schools for Neal and his siblings.

In 8th grade, Loving was assigned to be a school hall monitor. With time on his hands, he began writing poetry including a verse called "My Ambition: *If my dreams for the future prevail/I shall be flying your daily mail.*" Loving's writing talent was dismissed by his teachers, but like most things in his life, as an adult he proved his skeptics wrong.

In the 1920s, a series of events occurred that steered Loving to aviation. In 1926, he saw a De Havilland biplane fly over his West Detroit neighborhood, and he was awestruck. Three years later, Detroit City Airport opened at the intersection of Gratiot and Connor in Detroit, with the police having to stop traffic as a city street ran through one of the runways. For only six cents, Neal would ride out on the streetcar and watch the flight activity.

Loving read Charles Lindbergh's 1927 autobiography *We,* which detailed Lindbergh's cross-Atlantic flight, further stirring his fascination with flight. After he'd managed to save $5 for his first airplane ride at Detroit City Airport, he was hooked. But opportunities for African Americans in aviation were close to nonexistent, and his family had no money for flying lessons.

There were essentially no opportunities for African American men in the military service academies. At West Point, for example, there was one African American cadet in the class of 1936, and he was shunned all four years—no one would speak, eat, or room with him because of his race. That cadet, Benjamin Davis, Jr., went on to become the first African American general in the post-World War II U.S. Air Force.

As a young African American, Loving had to confront entrenched societal prejudice and discrimination. With the insurmountable odds against their son, his parents were not overly supportive of Neal's flying and encouraged him to learn a trade to support himself.

Loving's father, encouraged by the Detroit Welfare Department, opened an optometry business catering to low-income residents in 1932. Through his dad's business, Loving met African American aviator Don Simmons, President of the Ace Flying Club, a flight-training organization for black pilots. Though Simmons unfortunately died in a plane crash soon after they met, Loving developed a life-long friendship with the flying club's secretary, Earsly Taylor. Ms. Taylor's support was very beneficial to Loving over the years, and, as we will see, she played a significant role in Loving's personal life.

The Great Depression brought more challenges. In 1934, Loving worked for the Detroit Welfare Department cleaning alleys and streets. Every morning, he walked three miles to work, regardless of the weather, and suffered from frostbite on a particularly cold morning. A year later Loving started designing a bare-bones glider in the

Neal Loving—courtesy of Wright State University Special Collections and Archives.

basement of the family home, scraping together material and time to build this aircraft.

In 1936, the Works Progress Administration (WPA) was hiring people for the Detroit Recreation Department. Loving applied for a job teaching model airplane design but was initially rejected because of his race. He did not give up. He contacted local civil rights leader Reverend Horace White and Lebron Simmons, president of the Detroit Chapter of the Urban League. The WPA yielded and hired Loving — restricting his teaching to predominantly black students. The WPA job provided $85 per month, which he mostly gave to his mother, providing her first regular source of income in years.

In December 1937, Loving met Clinton Walker, the first African American in Michigan to obtain a private pilot rating. Through

Walker, he met instructor Paul Hinds, who was white and who defied the era's bigotry by providing flying lessons to serious-minded African American students. Loving's first solo flight occurred in April 1939. He also participated in activities such as a "Negro Aviation Week," where young people were encouraged to learn about flying and aircraft model building.

Loving's next step was starting a job at City Airport's Aero Mechanics High School in July 1941. Surprisingly, his class of mostly white students were very receptive to him, with no reported race-related issues. At this time, Loving organized the Wayne Aircraft Company on Detroit's Hastings Street and bought his first powered aircraft, a Waco.

America's entry into World War II prompted more changes in Loving's career path. Early on in the war, he applied to become a member of the Tuskegee Airmen but was rejected because he was near the age limit, did not have a college degree, and had failed a military medical exam because of a previously unknown heart condition. Undeterred, he contributed to the war effort by organizing Civil Air Patrol (CAP) Squadron 639-5, an all-black squadron.

Despite the entrenched racial barriers, he remained undeterred. Years later he reflected in his autobiography "Loving's Love":

"The wall of racial prejudice seemed at times impenetrable...with the support and encouragement of respected members of the black community, as well as influential whites such as George Tabraham (one of his instructors), I managed to achieve a measure of success many thought impossible."

Several years into World War II, Aero Mechanics High School lost their funding, and Loving had to take an entry level job as an engine assembler at Ford Motor. Meanwhile, he was still pursuing his interests in aviation, leading to a near tragedy on a July 1944 flight from Utica's Wings Airport.

Loving had worked the 3:00 p.m. to midnight shift the previous day. Fatigued, he made several errors in this flight, resulting in a stall and crash. He was lucky to be alive, but he survived at a steep price: he lost both legs below the knees and spent the next six months recovering in the hospital. On top of his lengthy and difficult physical recovery, Loving's mother passed away and his fiancée broke off their engagement.

Nevertheless, Neal Loving confronted his adversity with grit and determination. His hospital recovery was extremely difficult. He was fitted with the wooden protheses of the day, and despite frequent falls and painful blisters on his legs, he eventually relearned how to walk.

Walking was only his first challenge, however. How would he be able to continue flying? In 1946, he returned to Wings Airport, the same site where he'd suffered his devastating injuries. With an instructor accompanying him, Loving successfully flew the same sequence of events that led to his stall and crash two years earlier. This bold flight was an important milestone in his goal to regain his pilot's license.

Loving enrolled in Detroit's Wayne State University (WSU) in 1945, but dropped out (later resuming his studies in 1954) because of job responsibilities. Nothing came easy to Neal Loving. Although he did well on WSU's entrance exam, an enrollment counselor recommended Loving study liberal arts, telling him "you probably have no talent for aeronautical engineering."

This "advice" was just another obstacle to be overcome. In 1946, Loving opened the Wayne School of Aeronautics (WSA) at Detroit's City Airport, which was open to students of all races. In business for over ten years, WSA was likely the first black-owned aeronautics company, influencing many young people towards careers in aviation. Loving wanted access to City Airport; with support from the CAP, NAACP, and the Urban League, the airport's management finally agreed to WSA's presence.

Concurrent with operating his flight business, in 1947 Loving began designing a midget racer with reverse gull wings, named "Loving's Love." Aircraft design is a very complex process, especially for someone with little academic training. Loving was intrigued by pictures in aviation magazines of "midget" racers, which had to meet specifications from groups such as the Professional Racing Pilots Association (PRPA). These highly specialized, cutting edge aircraft could top 200 miles per hour.

This project required countless hours of work and knowledge of advanced mathematics to draft detailed plans—including an inverted gull wing. Loving researched all aspects of airplane design in fulfilling his one-man effort. He needed multiple drawings before starting construction, as well as using hundreds of linear feet of aircraft quality spruce wood. He constructed the aircraft in the basement of the Brewster Housing Project, in former Civil Air Patrol space.

Loving wanted to make the front of the aircraft as small as possible to reduce aerodynamic drag. One step in the process required taping paper to a wall in his workshop and then tracing his body outline on the paper. His next step was to form-fit a curve for the front of the aircraft to accommodate his size. The small cockpit, while sound for flying, restricted body movements and made flying very uncomfortable.

The racer was formally known as a WR-1, was approved by the PRPA in January 1948 and registered at Wayne County Airport as N351C. With help from friends, Loving disassembled the WR-1, nicknamed "Loving's Love," and moved it to Wayne Major Airport (now Detroit's Metro Airport) where it first flew on August 7, 1950. Because of mechanical problems, his plane never competed in aircraft racing. However, Loving was invited to join the PRPA—with membership card #104—without a doubt, Neal Loving was the first African American, double amputee, participant.

In December 1953, Loving flew "Loving's Love" over 4,500 miles round trip from Detroit to Kingston, Jamaica—a very long trip in a very small aircraft—with numerous stops along the way in the U.S., Cuba, and then on to Jamaica. In 1954, the WR-1 won the Most Outstanding Design award at an EAA fly-in convention. This aircraft is now displayed at the EAA AirVenture Museum in Oshkosh, Wisconsin.

By the mid-1950s, business at Loving's aeronautics school began dwindling. Returning veterans had used the GI bill for flying lessons after World War II, and many of those who were interested had already completed their schooling. After a successful decade, WSA closed after the 1957 flying season. Loving returned to WSU full time to become the school's oldest engineering graduate at the time, at age forty-five.

Despite his non-stop work schedule, Loving's personal life flourished. In 1955, he married Clare Barnett—sister of a friend and colleague from

Jamaica, Carl Barnett. Carl Barnett had married Loving's long-time business associate, Earsly Taylor. The Loving's adopted two children, Paul and Michelle, and moved to Yellow Springs, Ohio, in the early 1960s where he worked as a civilian specialist for the Air Force for twenty years at Wright Field in Dayton.

Loving's work at Wright Field focused on high-altitude clear air turbulence, and it took him to all corners of the world, working with projects including the Supersonic Transport and the U-2 spy plane.

Though busy with his demanding Air Force career and family obligations, Loving continued designing aircraft. He built two different "roadable" cars, which have the ability to fly and could be driven on a road. The first such car was a "WR-2," which had design flaws when flying. A new and improved version, a "WR-3," flew perfectly on its first flight in April 1968. This aircraft is now on display at the Smithsonian Museum in Washington.

Loving was honored as an "Outstanding Handicapped Employee" of the entire U.S. Air Force in 1968. One of ten finalists, the chaplain for the event told Neal the reason he did not win was because, "Everyone else had canes, crutches, wheelchairs…you walked across the stage as if you weren't handicapped at all…the least you could have done was limp a little bit!"

Loving retired from the Air Force in January 1982, receiving a letter from one of the senior officers at the base that include this personal acknowledgment: "Your leadership, knowledge, and technical ability will stand as a major record of excellence against which future engineers will be measured. Your high standards have contributed to a stronger national defense and a better Air Force."

At the encouragement of friends, this inspirational man wrote his auto-biography in 1994: *Loving's Love: A Black American's Experience in Aviation*. Loving provided an excellent account of his life story with his considerable writing talents, so often dismissed in his school days, on full display.

One of Neal Loving's most enduring legacies is as a teacher. He visited disabled children at the Roosevelt Institute in Warm Springs, Georgia. He kept in touch with students he taught at the YMCA, many of whom made significant contributions in a wide range of professions.

In a 1995 address to the National Management Association, Loving commented about his first business trip to Paris for the Air Force, noting that he was flying on a Boeing 707, similar to the route Lindbergh had flown in 1927—and how hard to believe this was for a kid growing up on Stanford Street in Detroit. He would often conclude his motivational talks by saying "the difference between the success or failure we experience as human beings is chiefly determined by how we...deal with our own special weaknesses."

Neal Loving received more than forty awards and honors for his outstanding work in many different aviation fields during his lifetime. He passed away in 1998.

This chapter first appeared as "Neal Loving: Flying Through Adversity" in *Michigan History,* a magazine published by the Historical Society of Michigan, Vol. 105 No. 2, March/April 2021 www.hsmichigan.org. Various edits have been made to the original article.

NINE

———————○———————

Rosie the Riveter Goes to Work— Then and Now

"Rosie the Riveter" is a great umbrella name for commemorating the limitless contributions of America's women production workers during World War II. These women pulled the same work load as the men they replaced (completing many jobs in the plants in addition to riveting)—all to produce the weapons and materiel that won World War II.

The *Rosie* name is best known in contemporary culture, other names used include *Wendy the Welder* and *Acetylene Annie*. Additionally, Women Ordnance Workers (WOWs) was a concept designed by the U.S. Army Ordnance Department.

However referenced, the need for women in munitions plants was driven by the huge growth of the United States military. In 1939, there were about 330,000 men in uniform; by war's end, over 12 million men were in military service. The resulting shortage of men in the civilian workforce was met by America's women—who dealt with inadequate housing and child care, tough working conditions, and limited receptiveness to women on the factory floor.

For purposes on this book, we will focus on aviation work completed by Michigan's Rosies at Ford Motor's Willow Run Bomber Plant, helping to assemble B-24 Liberator bombers. Over 8,600 B-24s were produced at Willow Run during the war. Women worked at a wide range of industries throughout Michigan and across the entire country on aviation and non-aviation production.

The challenges working women faced in U.S. defense plants during World War II were enormous. Reading or hearing their personal accounts provides a real appreciation of these difficult times. Long-term, the Rosies set the stage for significant societal changes, with women fully participating in what had been predominantly male roles.

The challenges for these women seemed to be unlimited, relating to every aspect of life. For example, inadequate housing was a constant problem. The influx of newcomers to work at Willow Run simply overwhelmed the available housing supply in the Ypsilanti area. In April 1942, there were approximately 8,000 workers at the plant with no available housing of any type within a 15-mile radius of Willow Run.

Local trailer parks did become available—with inadequate water, sewage disposal, and virtually no amenities. Housing construction was hampered by the lack of workmen and materials, which were needed by the military. The government built a variety of housing structures, such as Willow Run Village. This neighborhood in Ypsilanti Township, nicknamed "Bomber City," opened in March 1943, with rooms starting at $5 a week. Only vestiges of the Village remain today. Line haul buses, often referred to as "cattle cars," were available to transport employees to/from the plant.

The National Housing Agency constructed over 1,200 housing units in the former Nankin Township, now the City of Westland. This subdivision, known as Norwayne is still a thriving community and has been included in the National Register of Historic Places. Given the housing supply shortage, workers also boarded in homes in communities such as Belleville and Ann Arbor.

Assuming our "Rosie" was able to find housing, work in the Bomber Plant presented many challenges. The plant was an intimidating at 3.5 million square feet, equivalent to over sixty football fields. It was very loud and, as there was no air conditioning, very hot in the summer. Once a Rosie arrived at work, she faced constant risk of injury. There was no Occupational Safety and Health Administration in existence, and ergonomic considerations had not yet become a high priority in

Rosie the Riveter—courtesy of the Yankee Air Museum.

workplace design. The tools and equipment used proved to be hazardous and a reported ninety-six injury-related amputations were performed at the plant hospital.

Transportation was another issue. Detroit had many defense plants that paid wages similar to the Willow Run Bomber Plant and closer to the area's population base. Thus, in an era of gas and tire rationing, potential workers who owned a vehicle might see a long drive as a major obstacle to working at Willow Run.

All of the women dealt with, and largely overcame, the stereotypes of the day. Ford's archive records note that "the housewife (has) adapted herself magnificently to her new job…. watching her drive rivets on the center wing, the onlooker gained the impression that she possessed years of experience." On a light note, management in the plant's early days put up signage reading "Gentlemen, watch your language. There are women present." These signs then became: "Women, watch your language. There are gentlemen around here."

The name Rosie the Riveter is limiting, implying that all women did was rivet. In reality, the female workforce did virtually any job available. According to Ford's records, the first woman hired at Willow Run was Agnes Mengies (one source showed her last name as "Menzies") in February 1942. While Ms. Mengies's job was not described, many others are, and some fascinating individual stories about these women are available.

Rose Monroe, a riveter, was "discovered" by actor Walter Pidgeon on a goodwill tour of the plant and she was selected her for an appearance in a war bonds promotional film. Ms. Monroe, a widow, had moved to Michigan from Kentucky as a single mom. The movie that was produced was shown in theaters throughout the nation between feature films. After the war, Ms. Monroe had a series of jobs before founding and operating the Rose Builders construction company in Indiana.

Margaret Arnold, from Traverse City, Michigan, was a crane operator. As noted in "From Willow Run to World War II—Stories About Michigan People who Made, Flew, Flew on, or Worked on B-24's during WWII", by Bernice Miller Sizemore, Ms. Arnold recalled her perch high above the plant floor:

I climbed to the second or third floor balcony, up a ladder onto a catwalk, dropped into a six-foot square steel cage…handled streetcar controls which moved the crane across the 200-foot bridge that spanned the assembly bay. From the crane I lowered a three-foot hook at the command of men on the floor called "hookers," who attached loads to the hook with steel cables. It was practically a glamour job which required good depth perception, a sense of responsibility, and great care.

Jean Zaranko took a bus from Taylor, Michigan, to the plant six days a week. Her dad would drop her off at the bus stop, then pick her up after a long exhausting day. Ms. Zaranko became a riveter on the B-24's center wing, noting "I just loved being a riveter...doing something special for my country." She worked hard to ensure that every rivet "was just right," and if not, she drilled it back out. Ms. Zaranko had been working as an elevator operator in Detroit's Griswold Building before the war. With an intense desire to support the war effort, she told the employment office at Willow Run she was eighteen and altered her birth certificate from her real age of seventeen. Often, she and her co-workers left handwritten notes in the aircrafts' wings, which ground crews might find months later and thousands of miles away in the middle of a war zone.

Dorothy Haener, from New Boston, Michigan, was a B-24 inspector. Ms. Haener witnessed the hardships endured by female employees, leading her to be politically active for years in the United Auto Workers. She then became one of the founders of the National Organization of Women.

Carleton's Marge Haskins kept track of tooling dies used in plant equipment. Ms. Haskins worked day shifts while her mother, Florence Sutherland, worked the night shift as a riveter. Later in life, Ms. Sutherland blamed the loud riveting noise for her hearing problems. Her usual commute time was an hour, one way, from Carleton, with six people carpooling together. When Ms. Haskins got home at night, chores such as tending the coal furnace were waiting for her.

African American women faced additional challenges, given the prejudices and discriminatory hiring practices of the day. Louise Thomas, who passed a 120-hour riveting course at Detroit's Commerce School made several trips to Willow Run for a job, without success.

Ms. Thomas contacted one of Detroit's black newspapers, the *Detroit Tribune,* noting "If I were a white woman (I'd be working) at Willow Run…. riveting war weapons to help our nation win the war…. We, too, are Americans." It is not clear from the available literature if Ms. Thomas ever secured a job at Willow Run.

Ms. Anderson (first name not available) was one of the first black women hired at the end of 1942. Anderson supported her family and was facing eviction from Detroit's Sojourner Truth housing project for not paying her rent. Despite her training as an inspector, she applied to Willow Run for a job five times before being hired.

The United Auto Workers (UAW) provided support for African American men and women at Willow Run. The UAW developed a flyer stating in part: "Mr. Ford, Negro men and women will and must play their rightful part in winning the war." By the end of 1942, a few black women were hired; by April 1943 records show 290 black female employees out of 15,000 total female employment.

Given challenges such as these, there is no surprise that production quality was a problem. Charles Lindbergh, who provided substantial assistance in the early days of plant operation, noted in October 1942: "rivets missing, rivets badly put in, rivet holes started and forgotten, whole lines of rivets left entirely out," among other issues. As the workforce gained experience, and as the Army Air Forces slowed modifications, productivity and quality improved, leading to a bomber an hour coming off the line. The plant was recognized with an Army Navy "Excellence" Award in 1944.

The Rosies were a terrific asset to the war effort, but this was not their only contribution. Their critically import work began impacting societal views of the role of women and began influencing national policy. Of course, many of these debates continue through to the present day.

Child care: In 1941 Congresswoman Mary Norton (D, New Jersey) helped amend the Lanham Act. There was substantial concern about absenteeism by female employees to tend to their children. This 1940 law authorizing war related government grants was amended to allocate federal and local funds to various child care centers.

Popular culture: Rosie began appearing in various cultural outlets. The Norman Rockwell and J. Howard Miller "We Can Do It!" Rosie the Riveter posters used different women as models and portrayed them as strong working people. The 1942 Rosie the Riveter song by James "Kay" Kyser promoted the Rosies' contributions. While not specifically attributable to Willow Run, these provided the public with frequent reminders of the Rosies' many contributions.

Labor/management relations: The UAW had a closed shop agreement with Ford. Ultimately, Local 50 "The Bomber Local" was organized at Willow Run, covering most employees, male and female. Even though labor unions had agreed to no-strike clauses, wildcat strikes did occur. In fact, there were thirty-three such walkouts at Willow Run in 1943 alone. Thus, many women became familiar with labor union member- ships, job actions, and collective bargaining through their war work.

Equal pay for equal work: In a May 1945 analysis, the average wage for women was $1.14 an hour, which was within 5% of the $1.19 average that men earned. The difference is likely explained by the difficulty women had in obtaining supervisory positions in the plant, as well as job classifications that may have put women at a disadvantage. Implementa- tion of this concept continues to be part of political dialogue today.

War's end resulted in American servicemen being discharged from the military after 1945, requiring their reintegration into the civilian work force and a subsequent shrinkage of female workforce participa- tion. The baby boomer generation began with a societal norm of dad working and mom at home with the kids. The emergence of a powerful civil rights movement raised national awareness of discrimination and prejudice in society.

Readers will have their own opinions as to society's progress in dealing with many forms of discrimination, but there is little doubt the Rosies' work throughout U.S. defense plants, and throughout Michigan, contributed to societal changes for the better.

"Rosie the Riveter" was inducted in the Michigan Women's Hall of Fame in 2017, with five of the "Original Rosies," women who worked in the defense industry during World War II, in attendance. Rosies were honored with a Lifetime Achievement Award by the Michigan Women's

Tribute Rosies Alison Beatty (left) and Brenda Presnell at work—courtesy of
Pete Lerro Photography.

Studies Association; the nomination was submitted by Belleville's Yankee Air Museum.

The legacy of the Rosies is kept alive in many ways, including the
work of the American Rosie the Riveter Association (ARRA) and the
Willow Run Tribute Rosies (the two groups are not affiliated with each
other). ARRA was founded in 1998 by Dr. Frances Carter, who worked
in an Alabama defense plant during World War II. ARRA encourages
student education about the Rosie story as well as research into family
histories connected to Rosies. ARRA has chapters throughout the
country, including three in Michigan as of late 2020—Cheboygan and
Emmet County, Eastern Michigan WOW, and Michigan-Willow Run.

All three of the Michigan chapters have either a direct or indirect
aviation connection. For example, the Cheboygan and Emmet County
chapter focuses on honoring the construction of the U.S.C.G. Cutter
Mackinaw, on display in Mackinaw City. This cutter participated in

search and recovery efforts for Northwest Flight 2501 and a B-52 crash off of Charlevoix (chapter 15).

The Willow Run Tribute Rosies were formed in 2013. Tribute Rosie leader Alison Beatty notes: "The Rosies…pay tribute to the millions of women who paved the way for future generations of women to succeed in careers not previously accessible to them." Rosies typically dress in Rosie attire— bandana, work shoes, red socks, and a blue work uniform.

The Willow Run team participated in the Library of Congress's Veteran's History Project, an Oral History Program with women who worked in defense plants including Willow Run. Some of these recorded histories will become part of the Library of Congress digital records, helping future generations understand the many challenges these women faced. Jean Zaranko and Marge Haskins, both cited in this chapter, were participants.

While it may be difficult to measure the impact of the presentations and events held by either of these groups, there is little doubt it has been very significant. For example, at one event, a World War II veteran mentioned to ARRA and Tribute Rosie Jeannette Gutierrez (membership in the groups may overlap) that his favorite song from the era was "Don't Sit Under the Apple Tree" by the Andrews Sisters. Gutierrez began singing, and the veteran joined in, while standing up from his walker with tears in his eyes. No doubt this emotional moment gave observers that day some time to reflect on the sacrifices by the men and women of the World War II generation.

Bette Kenward is a Tribute Rosie and also leads the Eastern Michigan ARRA team. Her grandmother was a Rosie at Budd Industries making war munitions (among many other items, the plant manufactured B-24 wingtips). Years after the war, Kenward became friends with an original Rosie, Mary Maiuri, who worked at Detroit's Briggs Manufacturing plant. Kenward's interest gave Maiuri some real perspective on the value of her contributions and it is likely she will be passing the story on to future generations of the Maiuri family.

After a 2015 Tribute Rosies event, an Original Rosie who attended noted: "Thank you for an awesome day (that) you gave me…a highlight of my ninety-one years. I was proud to serve my country…Willow Run was a great place to work." Both of these organizations—ARRA and the Tribute Rosies—are helping keep these memories alive for future generations.

This article first appeared as "'We Can Do It!' Rosie the Riveter at Willow Run" in *Michigan History,* a magazine published by the Historical Society of Michigan, Vol. 103 No. 5, September/October 2019 www. hsmichigan.org. Various edits have been made to the original article.

TEN

Schlee and Brock
Try the Impossible

Charles Lindbergh's New York to Paris flight in May 1927 captured the imagination of the world and made Lindbergh world- famous. Three months after Lindbergh's trip, two men— Ed Schlee and Bill Brock— tried to fly around the world in an aircraft not much larger than Lindbergh's "Spirit of St. Louis" Ryan monoplane. In late August 1927, Schlee and Brock began this truly Herculean effort.

Detroit's Edward Schlee was born in 1887 and, with his brothers, formed the Wayco Oil Company after World War 1. Schlee and Wayco owned about 100 gas stations in metro Detroit. Schlee was also a pilot, and on one flight landed his aircraft on a golf course on Michigan's Mackinac Island. For a time, he also owned an air taxi service of Stinson bi-planes. His chief pilot was Bill Brock.

Ohio's William Brock was born in 1895. When he was fifteen, Brock traveled to Glenn Curtiss's flying school in Hammondsport, New York. Brock told Curtiss that he did not have the $150 tuition, so Curtiss told him to write home for funds; in the interim, working in the kitchen would be acceptable to cover board. Unknown to Curtiss, Brock had flying lessons (including stunt flying) from one of the instructors and was soloing in less than a week. Brock was a very good student —it did not take long before the instructor said, "Kid, you are as good as I am."

Brock gave Glenn Curtiss a ride, Curtiss was satisfied with the flight, and aviation history was in the making.

The mid-1920s was an era of aviation challenges. In April 1924, four Douglas World Cruiser biplanes, each with a two-man crew, began an around-the-world trip taking 175 days to fly almost 24,000 miles (two of the original four aircraft completed these flights). Lindbergh's May 1927 trip took less than 34 hours, earned him a $25,000 prize, and sparked even more interest in challenging (and very high-risk) over-ocean flights.

Advances in aviation technology were supported by many influential people of the day, such as the industrialist Henry Ford and his son, Edsel Ford. Based in Dearborn, Michigan, the Fords sponsored an annual "Ford Reliability Tour" to help build the public's trust in air travel safety. The first such tour was held in 1925. The 1927 tour, held from June 27 to July 12, covered over 4,000 miles within the United States and was won by the same aircraft that would be used by Schlee and Brock. Eddie Stinson, co-founder of Stinson Aircraft, was the pilot, accompanied by Schlee, Schlee's wife, and other passengers. Originally named "Miss Wayco" after Schlee's company, the aircraft was re-christened the "Pride of Detroit" for the round-the-world try.

Similar to Henry and Edsel Ford, Schlee wanted to prove the reliability of air travel. "Our flight is not a stunt. Our main purpose is to demonstrate, dramatically perhaps, but definitely, how practical and serviceable travel by air is today," he said. An additional goal was to beat the world-crossing record, which at the time was about twenty-eight and a half days. That effort was completed in 1926 by Linton Wells and Edward Evans, who used steamships, trains, cars, and aircraft for their multi-modal trip. Schlee and Brock's attempt would be 100% airborne.

Flying around the world with 1920s technology had many challenges. The flights would be costly, but Wayco's profits enabled Schlee to provide $100,000 of funding. He also organized the route and refueling, maintenance, and rest stops. These and other logistics took about a year to organize, dealing with slow communications, language translations, and foreign government bureaucracies. Assistance was promised by the United States Navy for the Pacific Ocean flight segments.

Ed Schlee and Bill Brock—Wikimedia Commons, Public Domain.

The crew needed a reliable aircraft. Stinson Aircraft built a variety of aircraft, including monoplanes such as the SM-1 Detroiter, which cost $12,000 off the assembly line. Depending on the configuration, the Detroiter held up to six passengers, was 32 feet long, had a wingspan over 45 feet, and was powered by a 220 horsepower Wright J-5 Whirl-wind engine. The Detroiter's maximum speed was 128 mph. The fabric wings were lacquered to tighten and stiffen this covering of the metal wing frames. The first Detroiter was manufactured in June 1927 at Stinson's Northville, Michigan, factory (aircraft were towed to a small airfield near Six Mile and Beck Road in Northville for flight testing).

All available cabin space would be used for fuel and oil storage. The instrument panel featured only the most basic instrumentation—various engine gauges, an air speed indicator, an altimeter, and an earth inductor compass. This compass was more stable than previous devices, making it easier to hold a heading over long periods in the air. Schlee and Brock did not have a radio onboard.

Concerned the Detroiter's loud engine would lull them to sleep, balsa wood was installed in the cabin to muffle the noise. Felt was placed over the gas tank in the fuselage for a bit of comfort during sleep time. Brock, who was short, thought he would have sufficient space but the taller Schlee would have to be a contortionist to fit in this limited area. The gas tanks were well sealed, although auxiliary five-gallon gas cans stored in the cabin likely would have led to exposure to gas fumes in the cockpit.

Plans were made to have an extra engine available in Tokyo, if they got that far and needed a replacement. A conversion table with time and distance on the axes, and data points for different air speeds, was carried for estimating the distance traveled. A description of various Japanese "aerodromes" was also available. One such facility, the Kasumigaura Aerodrome, was described as 1,800 x 1,000 yards, with a good runway surface and satisfactory workshops.

The Wright Whirlwind engine was a real asset for long-distance avi-ation efforts. The Wright was a nine-cylinder radial air-cooled engine, which weighed less than liquid-cooled engines as there was no radiator, coolant, and related hardware. The simpler and lighter design meant less could go wrong and the extra fuel that could be carried extending its range.

The official start point for the flight would be Harbour Grace, New-foundland. There was just one problem with this location: As of early

August 1927, there was no airstrip available. To rectify the situation, Stinson's Fred Koehler traveled to Newfoundland to meet with residents. A location near Crow Hill was selected as suitable land for an airstrip. City officials approved construction of the airstrip on July 25, 1927, with local citizens and the Newfoundland government making contributions. Work began in early August, with workers clearing an area about 4,000 feet long and 300 feet wide, and was finished shortly before the "Pride of Detroit" arrived. Extensive manual labor and horse-drawn carts were involved in hauling away rock and other debris from what became the landing field.

Schlee and Brock did not appear to be averse to publicity. A July 1927 letter from Warner Advertising indicated to Schlee that press releases had been sent to local magazines and other publications. Various advertisements promoting use of Shell gasoline were produced, as Wayco was a Shell distributor.

The aviators left the Ford Airport in Dearborn, Michigan, on August 23, 1927, with stops in New York and Maine before arriving at Harbour Grace (it is unclear why the flyers did not designate Dearborn as the "official" starting point). Brock was confident that they could complete the trip in under eighteen days—flying just over 22,000 miles in about 240 air hours—for an average speed of 92 mph.

Schlee and Brock took off from Harbour Grace on August 27 at 7:43 a.m. (local time), heading to England. After twenty-four hours of flying, they made landfall, but did not know where they'd landed. The coast could have been any of France, England, Wales, or Ireland. A message, weighted down by an orange, was dropped to a few onlookers at a small fishing village. The residents retrieved a large Union Jack flag, and the explorers were able to get their bearings once they realized they were over England.

Much more flying was ahead. After leaving England, stops included Germany, Yugoslavia, Turkey, "Irak" (Iraq), "Persia" (Iran), Pakistan, India, Burma, Indo China (Vietnam), Hong Kong, Shanghai, and Japan.

The travelers faced ongoing challenges. They could not find Stuttgart's airfield, which they later learned was fifteen miles south of the city, so they opted for Munich. In Hong Kong, they were faced with a

"Pride of Detroit" at the Henry Ford Museum—courtesy of the author.

very risky takeoff, as heavy rain the night before departure left the dirt field in poor condition—especially for a heavily loaded aircraft. Maintenance was also a constant concern. Once, after a day of flying, Brock spent over three hours fixing a magneto and adjusting tappet rods and rockers in the engine. Once that was completed, he took time to eat.

Neither of the men anticipated much rest during the flight; Brock noted: "If we get five hours a night, we'll be satisfied." Food would be whatever was available. Language was not a concern as "we know the motions and gestures." Brock did most of the flying; Schlee calculated drift and pumped gas from reserves into the main tanks.

Weather was an ongoing problem; the crew dealt with a gale in the eastern Atlantic, heat and dust in southern Persia, and severe storms in India and southeast Asia. Brock later stated the most dangerous part of the flight was a monsoon after leaving Shanghai. "We were tossed about unmercifully," he said. After leaving China, thunderstorms forced them down on "Kiushiu" (Kyushu) Island. When they reached Tokyo on Sept. 13, they had covered over 12,000 miles in nineteen days of travel with a flight over the Pacific still to be completed.

The cross-Pacific effort would be extraordinarily challenging and risky. After leaving Tokyo, the flyers would have had to find Midway Island—about 2,500 miles away. Midway primarily consists of two small islands, each about two miles long and a half mile wide, with a high point of 45' above sea level—essentially specks of sand in the ocean. After Midway, two more long-haul over-water flights would be required—1,440 miles to Honolulu and 2,400 miles to San Francisco—thus more than 6,000 miles of travel from Tokyo.

By this time in 1927, a series of tragedies had the public questioning transoceanic flying. Canadian aviators Terrence Tully and James Medcalf attempted a flight from London, Ontario, to London, England, in August 1927. At some point after leaving Newfoundland, the aircraft and crew disappeared into the Atlantic. In another tragedy, ten people lost their lives in the Dole Race, flying from California to Hawaii. The Navy spent millions of dollars searching for these lost fliers but abandoned the effort due to very limited budgets; the Navy then rescinded their offer to help Schlee and Brock. Navy Secretary Curtis Wilbur said the Navy department would no longer "aid and abet any man who attempted to commit suicide."

Meanwhile, hundreds of telegrams were sent to the U.S. embassy in Tokyo, pleading for the flyers to call it quits. Press and aviation experts began calling the trip a suicide flight. One telegram, received by the American Consul, was from Schlee's children Rosemarie and Teddy: "Daddy dear please take boat home to us we miss you." Schlee's wife hoped that the flyers would be "sensible and take a Vancouver boat."

Given this pressure, the trip was abandoned on September 15. Heeding Mrs. Schlee's advice, the two fliers took a passenger ship back to the United States, along with a partially disassembled "Pride of Detroit." Arriving in San Francisco, Schlee indicated public opinion (as well as the Navy's change of heart) influenced their decision "after we got about 800 cablegrams from friends and relatives telling us it would be suicidal...we decided to give it up."

The fliers had their aircraft reassembled in San Francisco and flew home. After several stops, they landed at Ford Airport in Dearborn on October 4. Friends and family hosted a parade and then a reception that evening, where Schlee collapsed from exhaustion.

Archive records show significant press coverage during the flight as information became available throughout the world. Locally, the *Northville (Michigan) Record* reported on September 9, 1927 "Stinson Plane Works Perfectly on World Flight" on page one. National and international coverage was provided by the *China Press, San Francisco Chronicle, Chicago Daily Tribune, New York Times,* and many others.

The *Detroit Free Press* provided this summary:

Schlee and Brock flew more than halfway around the world with only brief stops, traversing oceans and continents, mountain ranges and deserts, combating fierce storms in strange lands and waters. Their skill and courage never failed them and their machine proved staunch. They demonstrated the practicability of sustained, long-distance flying. All these things combine to make their trip "the greatest flight."

Schlee and Brock had a fair amount of celebrity after the flight. In an appearance in Lansing, Michigan, the message to attendees was "aviation today is safe, is sane, and practical." In 1928, Schlee sold the Wayco Oil Company, and used the proceeds for ventures such as the Schlee-Brock Aircraft Corporation, which, among other things, sold Lockheed Vega aircraft. The flyers took various long-distance flights around the country, but nothing compared to their cross-globe effort.

The air business fell victim to the Depression. In 1931, the "Pride of Detroit" was auctioned to satisfy a debt (at one point it was stored in a cow shed). The aircraft was subsequently restored and is now displayed at the Henry Ford Museum in Dearborn, Michigan, very close to the Ford Airport location used for the origin of the round-the-world flight attempt.

Bill Brock passed away from cancer in 1932 at age thirty-six. Ed Schlee worked as an aircraft inspector at Packard during World War

II and passed away in 1969. Their effort, along with those of countless men and women since their time, have led to tremendous advancements in aviation technology and safety. Round-the-world travel can now be completed in just a few days, with minimal stops, and with a level of comfort and safety that Ed Schlee and Bill Brock could only have imagined.

This chapter first appeared as "The Greatest Flight" in *Aviation History,* a magazine published by Historynet.com, Vol. 31, No. 4, March/ April 2021. Various edits have been made to the original article.

ELEVEN

Michigan Goes into Space

Jack Lousma and Roger Chaffee, Wikimedia Commons, Public Domain.

Michigan has a long and distinguished history of supporting the space program. This chapter focuses on astronauts Roger Chaffee and Jack Lousma, both from Grand Rapids, as well as several of Michigan's other connections to space exploration.

Roger B. Chaffee was born in February 1935, spending his earliest years were in Greenville, before a family move to Grand Rapids. His father, Donald Chaffee, was a barnstorming pilot who took seven-year-old Roger on his first flight over Lake Michigan—an early step towards an aviation career. Another of Roger's interests was engineering, writing at age fourteen in a 1949 school essay:

> I admire a person…that has ambition to make something of him-self, that does his work without crabbing…I chose electronics… because I have always liked to play with motors…(and) to play with and make radios. I feel that I can succeed because I like the subject, and I think that if you like the subject enough and if you try hard enough that you can succeed, and I certainly will try… It is still a subject in which you have an opportunity to really go a long ways and that's what I like.

Chaffee set up a small workshop in his family's basement for tinker-ing, experimentation, and building model airplanes with his dad. Always a high achiever, he became an Eagle Scout in Troop 215, to which President Gerald Ford had belonged to as a young man. An excellent student, Chaffee began college at the Illinois Institute of Technology; his next step was transferring to Purdue University in 1954, with a goal of becoming an aeronautical engineer. Chaffee enrolled in the Navy's ROTC program, earning his wings in 1957, and then married Martha Horn several days later. Among Chaffee's assignments was flying photo reconnaissance missions over Cuba during the 1962 Missile Crisis.

Chaffee could clearly see the moon on some night flights. Once President Kennedy announced a national goal of reaching the moon by 1970, he would reflect: "I've got to get up there. I've just got to get one of those (moon) flights." In 1962, NASA requested applications for four-teen available positions in their third astronaut class. Chaffee applied, and after a very difficult examination process, was selected out of a pool of 1,800 applicants. In October 1963, Chaffee returned from a hunting trip and had a phone message from NASA. He returned the call and was told he had been chosen as an astronaut and was later introduced to the public at a press conference in Houston, Texas.

Chaffee was assigned in March 1966 as one of the prime crewmen for the Apollo 1 mission—the first scheduled flight for the Apollo program. He began a very rigorous training program for this shakedown mission of a new spacecraft. Chaffee, of course, was not unaware of the risk he was taking. Flying jets from aircraft carriers was (and remains) a very high-risk profession; spaceflight presented many new dangers. In a late 1966 press conference, he remarked "There are a lot of unknowns of course, a lot of problems that could develop...they'll have to be solved and that's what we're here for. This is our business...."

Apollo 1 had very high visibility, as it was the first mission for the Apollo spacecraft and a key part of meeting Kennedy's man on the moon goal. NASA must have had an extraordinarily high level of confidence in all three Apollo 1 astronauts: Chaffee, Lt. Col. Virgil "Gus" Grissom, and Lt. Col. Edward White II (by this time in his career, Chaffee was a Lt. Commander).

Chaffee served in several roles in the buildup to Apollo 1's planned launch. Specializing in communications, he was involved with the Deep Space Instrumentation Facility—a series tracking stations for the space program in several worldwide locations. He served as Capcom for Gemini 4, crewed by Jim McDivitt and Ed White. Capcoms were the communications conduits to/from the astronauts and Mission Control. Grissom, no soft touch, had plenty of time to observe Chaffee's work and noted: "he's just a damn good engineer."

Tragedy struck when all three died in a January 1967 capsule fire in what was believed to have been a low-risk test, as the rocket boosters were not fueled. Apollo 1 had been scheduled to launch in late February 1967. The investigation into the tragedy led to many redesigns of the capsule and improvements in NASA processes, with the next manned Apollo launch occurring in late 1968. The changes made as a result of the tragic loss of Apollo 1 and its crew helped lead to Apollo 11's success and Neil Armstrong taking the first step on the moon in July 1969—six months ahead of Kennedy's deadline.

A fitting tribute to the Apollo 1 crew is a plaque on the launch pad where they perished reading "*ad astra per aspera,*" meaning a rough road to the stars. Chaffee is buried at Arlington National Cemetery, near Gus Grissom. Ed White is buried at West Point, having graduated from the Academy in 1952.

Memories of Apollo 1 and the loss of the three astronauts faded over time. Fifty-one years later, however, the Michigan Military Preservation Society (MMPS) swung into action. This group, a non-profit organization of veterans honoring historical contributions by West Michigan veterans, decided Chaffee deserved a full-scale bronze statue memorializing his life.

"He lived a short life, but he crammed a tremendous amount into it," said David Thompson, U.S.N. (Ret.). "Everybody liked Roger." Thompson attended Grand Rapids Central High School and was on the track team with Chaffee. Thompson chaired the statue project, along with MMPS board members Dan Pfeiffer and Bud Vierson.

The MMPS board approved the concept in 2015, choosing sculptor J. Brett Grill for the project. Grill's work included sculptures of President Gerald Ford and University of Michigan (U-M) Football Coach Bo Schembechler. Grill obtained many photos of Chaffee and visited the U.S. Space and Rocket Museum in Alabama to see examples of the space suit Chaffee would have worn—all to make the work as accurate as possible.

Thompson commented that it took about three years of effort to finalize arrangements with Grand Rapids. In early 2018, agreement was reached to place the Chaffee statue on the corner of East Fulton Street and Sheldon Avenue in downtown Grand Rapids, near the local Children's Museum.

The dedication ceremony and official unveiling of the statue was held in May 2018. Attending the dedication was Chaffee's widow Martha Chaffee, their children, Sheryl and Mark, and other family members and friends, such as David Pequet, Chaffee's nephew and the Treasurer of the Roger B. Chaffee scholarship program.

The scholarship program was established in 1967 in Chaffee's memory, and awards a $3,000 college scholarship each year to an outstanding high school senior in the local area. Awardees aspire to a college career in engineering or the sciences. So, in a very real sense, one of Chaffee's legacies are the accomplishments of these students. In a series of interviews for a biographical video of Chaffee, it is clear the engineering and science worlds are very well served by these scholars.

Another Grand Rapids native who left an imprint on the space program is Colonel Jack R. Lousma, born in February 1936. Lousma's father worked in Ypsilanti's Willow Run Bomber Plant as a riveter and in the power plant during World War II when the family moved to Ann Arbor. Lousma graduated from Ann Arbor High School, then earned an Aeronautical Engineering degree from the U–M in 1959. (Jak was a backup quarterback on the football team, until an arm injury ended his football career.) He married Gratia Smeltzer in 1956.

While at U–M, Lousma became interested in airplane design, aerodynamics, and flying. He was too late for ROTC enrollment, but did speak with two U.S. Marine recruiters, leading to his application to become a Marine pilot. Lousma graduated from U–M, made it through Boot Camp, and was commissioned as a Second Lieutenant, setting the stage for his remarkable career in aviation and as an astronaut.

After flight training, Lousma received his wings in 1960 and was assigned to Marine air squadrons in North Carolina, Puerto Rico, Guantanamo, and in Asia. While based in Japan he had to eject at low level into a lake when an engine failed. He sent a telegram home as international phone calls were then very expensive: "Ejected last night; parachute worked as advertised."

Lousma was intrigued by NASA and the astronaut program, but he thought NASA's approach to prospective candidates would be "Don't call us; we'll call you." He realized his error when he saw an advertisement in the base's weekly newsletter inviting Marine pilots to apply. Gratia was very supportive of his application. Lousma thought: "I wondered why she was so willing. She thought the same thing I did—10,000 people (would apply). Why start an argument, when I won't make it anyway?"

Both were incorrect in their assessment, as Jack was one of nineteen astronauts selected in the April 1966 astronaut class. He served in the support crews for three Apollo missions, but a lunar trip with Lousma on board was canceled after the space program scrubbed flights such as

Apollo 18. As Apollo 13's Capcom, he heard one of the most famous sentences in U.S. space history when astronaut Jack Swigert, Jr. said: "Houston, we've had a problem here." According to NASA's transcripts, Lousma asked Swigert to repeat what he'd said, as he had been talking to the flight supervisor; Swigert repeated the now famous phrase.

Lousma flew on two space missions after Apollo. The first was Skylab-3 with Alan Bean and Owen Garriott, which flew from July 28 to September 25, 1973. Skylab, which was America's first experimental space station, was designed to prove that humans could live and work in space for extended periods.

The astronauts flew 858 revolutions of the earth and traveled over 24 million miles in orbit. The crew made many repairs and upgrades on the spacecraft and completed work such as solar observations and medical experiments, and the crew overachieved by completing 150% of mission goals.

In an interview, Lousma noted that one of his more interesting experiences was a trip to Moscow. He had trained as a back-up for the Apollo-Soyuz Test Project, which included a number of trips to the Soviet Union for the U.S. astronauts. "We were there when President Nixon and Secretary of State Kissinger made a state visit. All of us astronauts and cosmonauts were part of that. It was a huge thing in (the Kremlin's) Saint George's Hall. We got to meet with Leonid Brezhnev and Alexei Kosygin."

Lousma's space travels resumed in 1982, when he served as Columbia's spacecraft commander (C. Gordon Fullerton was the pilot) on Space Shuttle mission STS-3. This eight-day spaceflight included exposing Columbia to extremes in thermal stress, using a fifty-foot remote manipulator system to maneuver a payload, and a wide range of scientific experiments. Columbia landed on a lakebed at White Sands, New Mexico, having traveled 3.4 million miles during almost 130 earth orbits.

Lousma retired from NASA and the Marine Corps in 1983 and worked in the private sector. He had a brief foray into politics, with a 1984 U.S. Senate run against Carl Levin. Lousma received 47 percent of the vote, a very respectable showing against an established incumbent.

In addition to his education at U-M, Lousma has a Master of Science degree in Aeronautical Engineering from the U.S. Naval Postgraduate School and has received honorary degrees from U-M, Hope College, and Cleary College.

University of Michigan and the Space Program

There are many other Michigan connections to NASA and the space program, including:

The June 1965 Gemini 4 mission was flow by NASA's first all-U-M crew: Ed White (eighteen months before Apollo 1) with a master's degree in aeronautical engineering, and James McDivitt, with a bachelor's degree in aeronautical engineering. McDivitt was born in Jackson, Michigan, and attended Jackson Community College, before matriculating at U-M. White became the first American to "walk" in space by exiting the spacecraft while in earth orbit.

After returning home, McDivitt and White were welcomed with a parade in Ann Arbor, receiving honorary doctorates of engineering in front of 30,000 Michigan Stadium spectators. A plaque designating the intersection of South and East University Avenues, near the Engineering Arch on Central Campus, was unveiled on the newly-named "McDivitt-White Plaza."

July 1971's Apollo 15 mission had a three-man "Maize and Blue" crew: James Irwin, Al Worden, and David Scott. Worden is a Jackson native. Irwin and Worden both earned two master's degrees in aeronautical engineering and instrumentation engineering, and Scott studied mechanical engineering at U-M before transferring to West Point. All three received U-M honorary doctorates after the flight.

The U-M connection of Apollo 15 led to a campus-wide legend that the crew left a "Block M" university flag on the moon. Not so, but the astronauts did leave a certificate on the Moon, reading: "This is to certify that The University of Michigan Club of The Moon is a duly constituted unit of the Alumni Association and entitled to all the rights and privileges under the Association's Constitution."

U-M Engineering Professor Harm Buning traveled to NASA's Johnson Space Center in 1963 to teach its first two "classes" of astronauts.

Buning later called it a "thrill" to discuss orbital mechanics with this "illustrious student body...I don't think I ever had a more dedicated and motivated bunch of students than on that occasion."

More from Michigan

Many other Michigan institutions and people have made substantial contributions to space exploration; a partial list includes:

Five Michigan universities—Central Michigan, Eastern Michigan, Northern Michigan, Siena Heights, and Wayne State—participate in the McNair Scholarship program. This program honors the memory of Dr. Ronald McNair, who was lost in the 1986 space shuttle Challenger explosion. These scholarships provide opportunities for young people to complete graduate school and doctoral research.

Michigan State University is home to the Abrams Planetarium, named in honor of Ted Abrams, and serves as an astronomy and space science education resource center.

Wayne State University—Eastpointe's Jerry Linenger has a doctorate from Wayne State. Linenger flew on the 1994 Discovery space shuttle mission, then spent five months on the Russian spacecraft MIR. Linenger completed the first space walk from a non-U.S. spacecraft and his 132-day space mission was at the time the longest by a U.S. astronaut.

All of the people mentioned in this chapter have received many awards and honors, and rightfully so. In a little more than 100 years of powered flight, Michigan's people and educational institutions have been at the forefront not only of aviation but in exploring the heavens.

TWELVE

Willow Run—Still on the Job

Willow Run, 2021—courtesy of the author.

Since the early 1940s, the Willow Run complex had been an integral part of Michigan aviation history.

In the 1930s this area was farmland straddling the Wayne/ Washtenaw County borders. Ford Motor owned over 1,400 acres of this property, including Camp Willow Run, which Henry Ford had built for boys whose fathers had been killed or injured in World War I. Willow Run Creek, a small tributary of the Huron River, flows through the area.

Farm use gave way to national defense needs. With the Axis Powers on the march in the late 1930s, government planners saw the need for accelerating war materiel production. President Franklin Roosevelt called for producing 50,000 aircraft a year at a time when U.S. output was a fraction of that amount. William Knudsen, then President of General Motors, was widely respected for his manufacturing knowledge and was appointed Chairman of the Office of Production Management, the federal government agency that coordinated wartime rearmament—an enormous responsibility. Knudsen was given wide powers to meet Roosevelt's ambitious goals; it was clear that all manufacturers in the Detroit area would be involved.

Detroit became known as the Arsenal of Democracy for its role in the U.S. outproducing Germany and Japan—a key factor in winning the war. Ford Motor's role is a microcosm of what all of the auto manufacturers and suppliers contributed to the Allied victory. Working on a government contract, Ford Motor built the Ford Army Air Force Plant #31 (referenced in this chapter as either "Willow Run" or "the plant") was built from the ground up. From 1942–1945, a total of 8,685 four-engine Consolidated B-24 Liberator bombers were produced at Willow Run. The total includes about 6,792 completed bombers and 1,893 "knockdown kits," which were sent to a Consolidated plant in Texas and a Douglas Aircraft plant in Oklahoma for final assembly. In total, over 18,000 B-24s were produced at five U.S. plants (more than any other U.S. aircraft type in World War II); Willow Run built more than any other location. Used worldwide, Liberators were likely best known for the August 1943 "Black Sunday" attack against the Ploesti, Romania, oil fields. Five Medals of Honor were awarded to pilots (three posthumously) for their deeds that day, which has never happened before or since in U.S. military aviation history.

One of the best-known Liberators manufactured at Willow Run was a B-24H model named "Witchcraft" and flown by the 467th Bomb Group at Rackheath in England. "Witchcraft" flew 130 combat missions without a mechanical turnback and did not have any crewmember wounded or killed when in action on this aircraft (this was at a time when air crew casualties were horrendous). "Witchcraft" returned to the U.S. and passed through Willow Run before being scrapped in late 1945.

The Willow Run plant's success was not pre-ordained. The original B-24 design was developed by Consolidated Aircraft in San Diego. In January 1941, Ford sent a team of executives to Consolidated, including President Edsel Ford and chief engineer Charles Sorensen, to review operations (also attending was Edsel's son Henry Ford II—a future company chairman).

It was clear Consolidated could not meet government requirements as their aircraft were essentially custom built and parts from one B-24 might not fit on another. Reuben Fleet, Consolidated's chief executive, did not appreciate the criticism of his operation from the Ford people and challenged them…how would you do it?

That night Sorensen sketched out the plant's overall design in his hotel room. His goal was to apply automotive mass production practices to aircraft. This was not a simple task as B-24s were far more complex than any automobile or airplane ever built in Detroit.

Ground breaking for the plant was in April 1941. By May 1942 an "Education Order" B-24 came off the line, which would be used for teaching purposes. By September 1942 the first production B-24 was completed, after taking about eighteen months to construct a functioning 3.5 million square foot plant. At one point, Willow Run was the largest aircraft manufacturing factory in the world; it was surpassed by a B-29 Superfortress plant in Chicago.

In the early days, the plant was derisively referred to as "Will-It-Run" given the poor quality of the B-24s produced. There were questions about the plant ever meeting its production commitments. Senator Harry Truman, who was leading a Senate investigation of defense contracting, visited along with other Senators and staff in 1942 to review the situation. Truman's committee criticized certain aspects of plant operations, but concluded that many of these problems were being resolved by 1943. Other distinguished visitors included President Franklin Roosevelt's 1942 inspection— including an uncomfortable ride through the plant with Henry Ford (the two had little use for each other). Aviators Charles Lindbergh and Jimmy Doolittle provided a wide range of technical advice.

A small sample of the hurdles dealt with includes:

- Virtually no blue prints or plans—In early 1941, about 200 Ford personnel were temporarily relocated to Consolidated to develop and transport blue prints to Michigan. This was no small task: as an example of the complexities involved a B-24 had five miles of electrical wiring.
- No flight test facilities existed for aircraft coming off the line, which led to the construction in 1941 of Willow Run Airport and of "Hangar One." Problems identified in flight tests would be fixed in this hangar. Once resolved, the aircraft were flown to Romulus Army Air Field (now Metro Airport) for delivery to the military; ferry pilots included Women Air Service Pilots.
- Endless changes from the military might stop production or require assembly line redesign. Army Air Force program management required over 500 B-24 modifications in Willow Run's first year of operations.
- Transportation infrastructure was very limited, leading to construction of the first highway triple overpass at Michigan Avenue/ Ecorse Road to ease the workers' commute. Rail spurs were built for equipment delivery such as Buick-built Pratt and Whitney engines and Ford-built tail assemblies. The Detroit Industrial Expressway (a forerunner of a portion of I-94) helped move aircraft parts from the Rouge complex to Willow Run.

While Sorensen had created the plant's concept, many operational details such as machinery layout, electrical, plumbing, and ventilation needed to be designed. Albert Kahn, the architect behind many well-known Detroit area landmarks, completed this work; Willow Run was his last project before he passed away. The plant contained four "tax turns," 90 degree turns at the end of the assembly line designed to keep the factory entirely in Washtenaw County, which had lower taxes than Wayne County. The plant was purposely built to accommodate manufacturing Boeing B-29s, but the war's end precluded the conversion effort.

B-24s were complex. Using rivets as an example, there were over 313,000 rivets in a single bomber installed at Willow Run (other rivets were on assemblies delivered to the plant; estimated total rivet counts/

aircraft vary widely). All were installed individually by human beings as no robot technology was available. There were over 500 rivet variants as the length, thickness, and composition differed based on each fastener's end-use. Distribution within the plant was an ongoing logistics challenge to ensure that workers got the right rivets at different points on the line.

Successful riveting required skill and was a two-person operation with one person holding a rivet gun and another a bucking bar. Rivets were driven into the bucking bar by air-hose powered guns—fixing together two pieces of metal. The air hoses caused constant vibration for the workers and a very loud plant.

Unsurprisingly, turnover was an endless problem given the difficult working conditions and the area's inadequate housing. Over 114,000 people worked at Willow Run from 1942–1945, with an average employment level of 27,000. Over 12,000 people quit in their first ten days on the job. In a pre-OSHA era, the plant was physically dangerous and the noise deafening. At its peak, over 42,000 people worked onsite, with many being be trained from the ground up. Approximately 40 percent of the work force was female; it was unprecedented to have women working in heavy manufacturing roles until World War II.

Ford claimed that a bomber an hour would come off the line; North American Aviation's President, James Kindelberger, said in a Detroit meeting this level of production was impossible. Yet by 1944, Ford met the bomber an hour goal—an incredible feat of manufacturing. However, aviation technology, particularly in wartime, moves quickly. B-24s had become obsolete by war's end. The final Willow Run built Liberator was produced on June 28, 1945. Shortly thereafter, Ford began laying off employees as the contract was cancelled.

Historian Victor Davis Hanson has commented on America's industrial might in World War II and how "successful captains of industry created huge factories, focused on a few models of…bombers, mass produced them on assembly line principles—and constantly demanded that extraordinary rates of production be further increased," capturing Willow Run's essence. Willow Run's aviation contributions have continued to the present.

Kaiser-Frazer and General Motors

In 1947, Kaiser-Frazer Automotive, a consolidation of companies operated by auto manufacturer Joseph Frazer and ship builder Henry Kaiser, obtained the plant. Kaiser-Frazer produced over 700,000 automobiles before running into financial difficulties. While Kaiser-Frazer focused on autos, the plant also produced 71 C-119 "Flying Boxcars" aircraft for Fairchild Aircraft.

As Kaiser-Frazer's fortunes were declining, a General Motors (GM) transmission plant in Livonia was destroyed in an August 1953 fire. This was critical for GM as the vast majority of their automatic transmissions had been produced at the destroyed plant. GM leased Willow Run and then went to work, redesigning the plant floor layout in seventeen days. About 2,500 personnel alternated ten-hour shifts to make the plant functional, and within twelve weeks, production resumed.

Willow Run's primary purpose for GM was building automatic transmissions— 82 million units came off the line for GM, with the last one being produced in 2010. An aviation connection remained as Willow Run produced M39A1 automatic cannons for aircraft such as the North American F-100 Super Sabre. GM also constructed another manufacturing plant, Willow Run Assembly, on the complex, producing vehicles such as the Chevrolet Corvair. Production ceased in 1993 after assembling seven million vehicles.

Air Freight

Willow Run was the base for many air freight businesses. Some are no longer in business, including Zantop, Trans Continental, Murray Air, Fleming International, and Rosenbalm. This chapter highlights Zantop and two current operators—USA Jet and Kalitta Air.

The year 1946 saw brothers Lloyd, Duane, Howard, and Elroy Zantop form "Zantop Flying Service" in Jackson, Michigan, to provide flight lessons. Family lore notes the brothers borrowed $1,500 to begin operations. Early on, Zantop hauled freight for GM, then expanded to Ford and Chrysler. Operations moved to Metro Airport in 1953, and the family sold their holdings in 1966. The Zantop family then returned to Willow Run in 1972 with Zantop International Airlines (ZIA), another air cargo venture. ZIA was once one of the world's largest cargo airlines and might carry a million pounds of freight a night.

Former employees have many fond, and sometimes colorful, memories of their ZIA days. Pilot Bill Travis recalled his hiring by ZIA from a local flight school in his book *Pan Am Captain Aiming High*, with the job offer from the Chief Pilot as follows:

Chief Pilot: "You're Hired; Now here's what you need to do—Go downstairs and get on the airplane that's getting ready to take you and other new hires to get your three take offs and landings. Come back up here to get two hours of ground school. Tonight, you'll report at 9:00 p.m. for an 11:00 p.m. flight to Saint Louis."

Travis: "I have a student scheduled in two hours and can't do this today."

Chief Pilot: "Do you want the fricking job?"

Travis: "Yes."

Chief Pilot: "Then get your ass on that airplane, or you won't get the job."

Travis found another instructor for his student and reported to work.

Although ZIA's primary business was freight, business executives and celebrities might charter flights. Flight crews could remove cargo liners and install seats in less than an hour as part of the freight/passenger conversion. One crew flew the rock group Crosby, Stills, Nash, and Young to a concert with the pilot and copilot receiving backstage passes for the show.

ZIA found the competitive environment increasingly difficult to navigate and ceased operations in 2005. Some of their aircraft remain in service with companies such as Buffalo Airways in Yellowknife, Northwest Territories, Canada.

Willow Run is still a major air freight airport; about 200 million pounds of freight pass through annually. USA Jet is one of the freight operators now at Willow Run. The company's founding goes back to Robert Phelps, who started as a Metro Airport mechanic in 1960—at $2/hour. Phelps went into business, opening Active Aero in 1979 at Willow Run (he since has sold his holdings, and there have been several reorganizations). USA Jet is part of the Active Aero Group, which in turn is owned by Ascent Global Logistics.

Former employee Jim Redick, Jr., recalled his time at the company in the 1980s. USA Jet had very limited staff, so Redick did just about everything on a typical night: taking customer calls, fueling the planes, pulling flight manifests and weather reports for the pilots, and loading cargo. Hours were irregular; night and weekend work were routine. A 2001 *Air and Space* article indicated not much had changed from the 1980s for USA Jet. Flights might be scheduled with very little notice; pilots sometimes slept in various Willow Run buildings. Pilots carried beepers and were expected to be at the airport ready to fly within twenty-five minutes of being paged. Shower facilities at the Willow Run Fire House could be used if needed.

Once airborne, the flight crews might experience additional challenges. In-air mechanical problems, bad weather, and dealing with customs on international trips were frequent concerns. Crews might also serve as cargo loaders—using heavy duty mitts, hooking cargo straps to pallets, and, along with a fork lift driver, loading the aircraft. Fuel load was another worry; a standing joke at USA Jet was "the only time you have too much gas is when you're on fire."

Today, USA Jet uses state-of-the-art technologies to meet customer needs—a logical extension of all the innovations introduced in the B-24 days.

Another significant Willow Run operator is Kalitta Air. Founder Conrad Kalitta grew up in Mt. Clemens, and began his air freight career flying parts for Ford Motor in a twin-engine Cessna. From this modest beginning, Kalitta, using various companies, grew into American International Airways (AIA), once one of the world's twenty-five largest airlines.

After a merger with another freight operator, Kalitta resigned from AIA to run an airline leasing business. Further organizational changes occurred, AIA went out of business, and operations resumed as Kalitta Air in 2000 with an extensive fleet of Boeing 747 and 767 aircraft.

Kalitta Air has been associated with key events in U.S. history. After the September 11, 2001 terrorist attacks, virtually all U.S. civilian aircraft were grounded by the FAA. Once exception was a Kalitta Air flight, departing Los Angeles at 1:21 a.m. (Pacific Standard Time) on September 12 with Red Cross disaster relief including about 50,000 pounds of blood, platelets, and other supplies. The flight was bound for Philadelphia; the supplies would be delivered to New York City or Washington, D.C.

FedEx Custom Critical initiated the flight when contacted by the Red Cross to find a company able to undertake this mission on short notice; Kalitta Air got the call. "The only question for us was if we had planes and people in Los Angeles, which we did," said Conrad Kalitta. All six Kalitta Air pilots who were in Los Angeles that day volunteered for the late-night flight. Another exception was provided by the FAA for USA Jet with similar disaster relief.

In 2003, Kalitta Air was awarded a Certificate of Appreciation for supporting U.S. military efforts in Iraq. In 2020, Kalitta Air flew evacuating U.S. citizens home from Wuhan, China, in a specially converted aircraft designed to limit further spread of the coronavirus.

As Ralph Fritsch, a crew member on the September 2001 flight, observed, "Where there's death, destruction, and mayhem, usually there's a Kalitta aircraft nearby doing something to help."

In addition to his business success, Connie Kalitta is a larger-than-life character. Consider an attempted hijacking in October 1989: A knife-wielding would-be hijacker walked into the company's Willow Run headquarters, wanting to rent a jet to fly to Washington, D.C. and "visit" the White House. Kalitta emerged from a meeting and agreed to fly this individual to Washington. His plan was to depressurize the jet at altitude and render the hijacker unconscious. Kalitta and a Michigan State Police trooper ultimately subdued the hijacker; Kalitta, who had minor injuries from this incident, returned to the meeting.

In addition to his aviation career, Conrad Kalitta had a long-time interest in automobile drag racing, and he was inducted into the Motorsports Hall of Fame in 1992.

All of the air freight operators at Willow Run experienced a cyclical business dependent on the auto companies and their highly variable sales. Other challenges were constant—services such as UPS and FedEx were formidable competitors. The auto companies began consolidating manufacturing facilities and suppliers began locating near these plants, reducing air freight needs. Military contracts began winding down after the Cold War.

Passenger Service

Passenger service is another part of Willow Run's story. The first airline flying into Willow Run was Capital Airlines-PCA in June 1946; metro-Detroit passenger service had previously been based at Detroit's City Airport. Other airlines followed, including American, United, North Central, Eastern, Northwest and TWA. Eventually, Willow Run became Detroit's primary airport.

The terminal was constructed inside Hangar One, originally built with eight maintenance "bays" for B-24 work. After the war, Bays 3 and 4 were converted into the passenger terminal; Bays 1, 2, and 5 handled baggage; and Bays 6, 7, and 8 handled maintenance. The terminal was sometimes referred to as "The Barn," given its bare-bones nature (period photographs suggest the nickname was appropriate). Architect Minoru Yamasaki was hired in the mid-1950s to update the terminal; later in his career, Yamasaki designed New York City's World Trade Center.

Willow Run had "Red" and "Blue" Concourses; passengers would board from a covered walkway, using stairs to reach their aircraft. An observation deck was built for public viewing of airport operations. The "Willow Run Airport Hotel" was in the mezzanine and an onsite movie theater could keep passengers occupied while waiting for a flight. "Radio equipped" busses took passengers to Willow Run from Detroit, allowing the terminal to be called if the bus was delayed and potentially changing flight schedules.

In the late 1950s, a passenger business competitor emerged—Detroit-Wayne Major Airport began promoting their location as a Willow Run alternative. By 1958, a new terminal and a longer runway were built at the now-renamed Detroit Metropolitan Wayne County Airport. The airlines began moving operations to Metro, and the last Willow Run commercial flight was in 1966.

Unique Aviation Stories

Willow Run has had its share of unconventional stories:

The rental car industry was boosted by Warren Avis, a World War II pilot who was often frustrated when ground transportation was not readily available at airports. He founded Avis Rent-a-Car in 1947 with one of the first airport outlets at Willow Run.

An Amelia Earhart commemoration flight took off from Willow Run in 1967—thirty years after Earhart and her navigator, Fred Noonan, disappeared near Howland Island in the Pacific. Schoolteacher Anne Pellegrino was part of a four-person crew, along with Lee Koepke, Bill Payne, and Bill Polhemus. All four were licensed pilots and took turns flying Koepke's Lockheed Electra; which was similar to the aircraft flown by Earhart.

The crew flew from Willow Run to Oakland, California, (Earhart's starting point), then headed east, flying over Howland Island on July 2, 1967, thirty years to the day after Earhart's planned arrival. Pellegrino dropped a wreath from the aircraft while Koepke held her, so she would not fall out the aircraft's open door. By mid-July, all four had flown back to Willow Run.

Military research was also completed at Willow Run. The Packard Hangar, on the east side of Willow Run was built during World War II; Packard conducted jet engine research in this building. In 1946, the University of Michigan (U-M) acquired the airport from the federal government for $1, which included a requirement for U-M to use the facility for research. The Michigan Aeronautical Research Center (MARC) was established. MARC separated from U-M in 1972 and became the Engineering Research Institute of Michigan. The U-M used several different Willow Run structures, including Hangar One, two "round-top" hangars (with curved roofs), the Packard Hangar, and Hangar 2041, which became the Yankee Air Museum's original home (see below).

One research initiative carried out at Willow Run was project WIZARD, which studied defenses against ballistic rockets—similar to the V weapons Germany used against England late in World War II. The program helped produce the BOMARC (combining Boeing and MARC) missile, which had its first production flight in February 1955. U-M resold the Airport to Wayne County in 1977—for $1.

A Douglas A-4C at Yankee Air Museum—courtesy of Melissa Workman.

Yankee Air Museum

The museum's origins go back to 1981, when local aviation enthusiasts such as Dennis Norton began considering a B-24 project. Given the B-24's history with Willow Run, why not bring a B-24 "back home" for display? This vision evolved into developing a museum for showcasing Willow Run's history—no small challenge.

Establishing such an organization meant finding volunteers, funding, a name, a Board of Directors, as well as a physical location. Norton, who became Museum member #1, approached the Wayne County Road Commission about obtaining Hangar 2041. This structure was used during World War II to train B-24 support crews and was available on Willow Run's east side. The Road Commission, which managed certain airport properties at the time, provided the hangar at no cost to the museum. As it turned out, the price was appropriate—virtually everything inside this unheated structure needed replacement or repair. After many hours of hard work, May 1982 saw the hangar's dedication as a home for the Yankee Air Force. Over time, the name evolved to the Yankee Air Museum.

During the 1980s, the Museum purchased three flyable aircraft—a Boeing B-17 Flying Fortress, a North American B-25 Mitchell, and a Douglas C-47 Skytrain (the military version of the DC-3). Over time, museum personnel acquired a fleet of flyable and static aircraft, undertook numerous restoration projects, and became a significant presence in the community. A disaster struck on October 9, 2004 when a fire of unknown origin destroyed the hangar, aircraft, artifacts, equipment, tooling, and many of the organization's records.

Quick-thinking volunteers on site when the fire began towed and pushed the B-17 and C-47 out of the burning structure; the B-25 was not in the hangar at the time. Acting swiftly, and at considerable risk to their own safety, their bravery saved these aircraft and likely the museum's future. Members decided to rebuild at an emergency meeting the next day.

News of the fire quickly spread in the aviation community. One of the aircraft destroyed was a North American Rockwell OV-10; the following excerpt summarized exactly the museum's approach to its post-fire future.

> While the loss of so much irreplaceable history at the museum is heartbreaking, we are encouraged to know that it's not as simple as "game over." The volunteers that keep a museum such as the Yankee Air Force going are a special breed of folks, who couldn't do what they do if they were easily deterred by adversity. These folks view "impossible" odds not as a deterrent, but as a challenge to be met with enthusiasm.

Since the fire, the Yankee Air Museum's staff and volunteers have continued moving forward with a wide range of actions. A partial list includes:

- Moving to its current location on Willow Run's east side in 2010 after using several temporary facilities.
- Purchasing 144,000 square feet of the Willow Run Bomber Plant in 2014 (the remainder was torn down; General Motors did not need

the capacity from this facility). Future plans for the plant are under development and the facility is primarily used for aircraft storage.

- Acquiring several new aircraft for display such as a McDonnell Douglas F/A-18 Hornet, which had previously flown with the Navy's Blue Angels. McDonnell Douglas was later acquired by Boeing, and the Museum's aircraft is so labeled.
- Adding two new flyable aircraft: a Bell UH-1 "Huey" helicopter and a Ford Tri-Motor.
- Continuing to host the annual *Thunder Over Michigan* airshow, a summertime staple in Southeastern Michigan. The airshow is manned by museum staff and volunteers, with varying themes each year; 2021's airshow featured B-25 Mitchell bombers.

A significant challenge emerged in 2018. Wayne County Airport Authority, the managing authority for Willow Run Airport, decided to decommission Hangar One for aviation purposes. As a result, all tenants needed to vacate, and the museum would have to find another home for its flyable aircraft operations and maintenance. As a result, the Museum decided to construct a new 36,000 square foot hangar near the existing museum. With an expected completion date of late 2021, the facility will be named the "Roush Aeronautic Center," in honor of long-time supporter Jack Roush. Museum leadership is confident guests will have a great visitor experience seeing the flyable collection close-up.

Eighty+ Years of Aviation History

The Willow Run complex has been a center of Michigan's aviation history since the early days of World War II, and the Yankee Air Museum has been commemorating history onsite for forty years. While both the airport the and museum continue to evolve, Willow Run and the Yankee Air Museum will remain an integral part of Michigan's aviation history for years to come.

THIRTEEN

○

The Kettles Aviation Legacy

Charles Kettles in Vietnam—Wikimedia Commons, Public Domain.

Visitors to Frankenmuth's Military Heroes Museum will find a display honoring Ypsilanti's Charles Kettles—no surprise as Kettles had an extraordinary life story of contributions to his country and to aviation history. Museum visitors will also find an additional display honoring Charles's father, Albert Grant Kettles. It is somewhat atypical to say the least to see a father/son aviation combination so honored.

The Kettles' story was intriguing and led to a research project to learn about their history. That research revealed that Richard Kettles—another of Albert's sons—made his own very significant contributions to Michigan aviation.

Albert Kettles

Albert Kettles was born in Bruce Mines, Ontario, in 1898. When World War I began, he joined the Royal Flying Corps-Canada and was sent into combat in Italy. Assigned to the 66th Squadron, he was credited with downing an observation balloon, which was considered the equivalent of four aircraft kills, as balloons were very important to the Central Powers' military.

Returning to Canada in 1919, Albert married Cora Stobie in 1924 and moved to the United States. He worked for Dodge and, on a part time basis, gave flying lessons in Detroit. In 1927, he became a pilot with SKF Flying Service in Lansing, which provided aviation support services at Capital City Airport. Kettles also served as station manager for Kohler Airlines, station agent for Pennsylvania Central Airlines, test pilot for Driggs Aircraft company, and as a pilot for the State of Michigan.

Kettles became the State of Michigan's first Chief Pilot in 1934 and one of the first instrument qualified pilots in the state in 1938. He volunteered for the Air Transport Command, part of the Army Air Corps, at Romulus on the day after Pearl Harbor. Commissioned as a Captain, and as one of the very few instrument qualified pilots available, he was frequently assigned to lead flights over the Atlantic Ocean. He flew Secretary of State Cordell Hull to a 1943 conference in Moscow that included British Foreign Secretary Anthony Eden and Soviet Foreign Minister Vyacheslav Molotov.

Kettles briefly served as Ford Motor's Chief Pilot after the war. In 1947 he became Chief Pilot for Abrams Aerial Survey in Lansing, one of the leading aerial photography companies in the world until his 1966 retirement. "I've been fortunate to be teamed with (Albert Kettles) who I respected so much" noted long time Abrams Survey Company employee Wayland Mayo (who had his own distinguished career in aerial photography).

Albert Kettles passed away in December 1972.

Richard Kettles

One of Albert's children, born in 1928, was Richard "Dick" Kettles who made his own mark on Michigan aviation. In 1962, he and his partners (including Mike Dow, current Chairman of the Alden and Vada Dow Family Foundations in Charlevoix) formed General Aviation, a Fixed Base Operator (FBO) at Capital City Airport. Kettles was the Company's President. FBO's provide aviation services such as fueling, hangaring, aircraft rental and maintenance, and flight instruction. General Aviation had at various times a Beech Aircraft and a Cessna dealership. New and used aircraft were sold and charter flights were offered to the public.

One day Kettles went to Dow with a "crazy" idea, believing an old Waco biplane could be built as new. This apparently farfetched idea led to the formation of Classic Aircraft, which helped keep alive Waco Aircraft's historic aviation legacy. Waco (originally Weaver Aircraft Company) produced some of the most popular aircraft of the 1920s and 1930s. The anticipated postwar boom in airplane demand did not materialize, and Waco Aircraft was out of business by 1947. Its aircraft type certificates and related drawings were donated to the Smithsonian Institute in Washington D.C.

Actually building new WACO's★ was not a simple proposition, even with the Smithsonian's information. Generally, the Federal Aviation Administration (FAA) never allowed building new aircraft with old plans and specifications. Kettles and Dow, however, created Classic Aircraft (at Capital City Airport) in 1983 with that very goal in mind. They visited the Smithsonian and reviewed archive records, finding the original type certificates and a complete set of Waco YMF-5 records. These aircraft were radial-powered biplanes with seating for a pilot and two passengers.

YMF-5s turned out to be an excellent choice for this project. Some pilots in *Flying Magazine* believed the 1935-vintage YMF-5 was the "most beautiful and desirable sport aircraft ever built." Old time aviators were receptive, and another selling point was the availability of WACO-compatible engines.

The team met with the FAA in Chicago, whose representatives initially wanted the old plans and specifications followed to the letter. Kettles suggested that certain changes, such as upgrading the original aircraft wings from cotton fabric to a more water-resistant material, be approved. The FAA realized the validity of Kettle's request, agreed with these changes, and ultimately provided production certificates that reflected the outstanding quality control at Classic Aircraft.

The first "next gen" of WACO's returned to the skies in November 1985. Kettles and the Classic team went from tooling to the first flying aircraft in nineteen months—five months better than the original twenty-four-month schedule. For many years, Classic Aircraft was the only FAA certified aircraft manufacturer in a seven-state area.

Classic was producing about ten aircraft a year by 1993, each plane requiring about 5,000 labor hours. Individual aircraft were customized based on customer request. Many of the workers came from a nearby GM plant, which had suffered heavy layoffs in the early 1980s. Kettles wanted to help by hiring some of these displaced workers; he also brought in Piper and Taylorcraft workers for their aviation manufacturing expertise.

The customer base for these specialized aircraft included Thomas Watson, Jr., of IBM (who had been IBM's President from 1952–1971), and Phillippe Kahn who invented the camera used in cell phones. Dick's son Donald Kettles was the sales manager and said: "You gotta love airplanes to do this...and you can't build anything this nice unless you're having fun."

In 1999, Dick Kettles sold his share of the business, which moved to Battle Creek and operates today as WACO Aircraft Corporation. Kettles could have received a higher sales price from another purchaser, but declined against that buyer because their plans would have relocated the company out of state—costing WACO's existing employees their jobs.

Dick Kettles many contributions were recognized when he was granted an Honorary Doctor of Science in Business Administration degree from Cleary College. He passed away at age eighty-seven in July 2015 in Lansing.

Charles Kettles

Another of Albert's children, Charles Kettles, was born in Ypsilanti in 1930. As a youngster, he attended the Edison Institute in Dearborn, Michigan, which is now part of the Henry Ford Museum. He attended Eastern Michigan University and had worked as an American Airlines baggage handler at Willow Run. Drafted into the Army, Charles graduated from the Army Aviation School in 1953, and served in Korea, Japan, and Thailand. After leaving active service he went into business with his brother and owned a Ford dealership in Dewitt. Charles and Dick were the youngest franchisees in company history.

Charles Kettles answered the call to serve again in 1963 when the Vietnam war was ramping up and helicopter pilots were needed. The helicopter war in Vietnam was intense and brutal. Bell UH-1 helicopters (generally known as "Hueys") were ubiquitous, serving in a wide range of roles. About 7,000 Hueys saw service in Vietnam, with very heavy casualties among the flight crews.

For all of the terrible losses during the war, there is no doubt the helicopter pilots' extraordinary flying skills and their crews' limitless amounts of courage saved many lives. Helicopters allowed for the quick transit of wounded service personnel back to field hospitals, as well having medics administer first aid while flying to a field hospital. Thus, the survival rate of wounded soldiers improved compared to Korea, which had limited use of helicopters.

Several helicopter pilots received the Medal of Honor for their actions in Vietnam, including Kettles. Kettles actions on May 15, 1967, originally earned him the Distinguished Service Cross (DSC). The DSC is the military's second highest decoration and was awarded to Kettles in 1968. This award was upgraded to the Medal of Honor by a special Act of Congress in 2016.

The Medal of Honor Citation follows:

For conspicuous gallantry and intrepidity at the risk of his life above and beyond the call of duty:

Major Charles S. Kettles distinguished himself by conspicuous gallantry and intrepidity while serving as Flight Commander,

176th Aviation Company (Airmobile) (Light), 14th Combat Aviation Battalion, Americal Division near Duc Pho, Republic of Vietnam. On 15 May 1967, Major Kettles, upon learning that an airborne infantry unit had suffered casualties during an intense firefight with the enemy, immediately volunteered to lead a flight of six UH-1D helicopters to carry reinforcements to the embattled force and to evacuate wounded personnel. Enemy small arms, automatic weapons, and mortar fire raked the landing zone, inflicting heavy damage to the helicopters; however, Major Kettles refused to depart until all helicopters were loaded to capacity.

He then returned to the battlefield, with full knowledge of the intense enemy fire awaiting his arrival, to bring more reinforcements, landing in the midst of enemy mortar and automatic weapons fire that seriously wounded his gunner and severely damaged his aircraft. Upon departing, Major Kettles was advised by another helicopter crew that he had fuel streaming out of his aircraft. Despite the risk posed by the leaking fuel, he nursed the damaged aircraft back to base.

Later that day, the Infantry Battalion Commander requested immediate, emergency extraction of the remaining 40 troops, including four members of Major Kettles' unit who were stranded when their helicopter was destroyed by enemy fire. With only one flyable UH-1 helicopter remaining, Major Kettles volunteered to return to the deadly landing zone for a third time, leading a flight of six evacuation helicopters, five of which were from the 161st Aviation Company. During the extraction, Major Kettles was informed by the last helicopter that all personnel were on board, and departed the landing zone accordingly. Army gunships supporting the evacuation also departed the area.

Once airborne, Major Kettles was advised that eight troops had been unable to reach the evacuation helicopters due to the intense enemy fire. With complete disregard for his own safety, Major Kettles passed the lead to another helicopter and returned to the landing zone to rescue the remaining troops. Without gunship, artillery, or tactical aircraft support, the enemy concentrated all firepower on his lone aircraft, which was immediately damaged by a mortar round that shattered both front windshields and the chin bubble and was further raked by small arms and machine gun fire. Despite the intense enemy fire, Major Kettles maintained control of the aircraft and situation, allowing time for the remaining eight soldiers to board the aircraft. In spite of the severe damage to his helicopter, Major Kettles once more skillfully guided his heavily damaged aircraft to safety. Without his courageous actions and superior flying skills, the last group of soldiers and his crew would never have made it off the battlefield. Major Kettles' selfless acts of repeated valor and determination are in keeping with the highest traditions of military service and reflect great credit upon himself and the United States Army.

The Medal of Honor (MOH) is the highest decoration given by the U.S. Armed Forces and is granted for valor in combat. More than 3,400 U.S. service members have been awarded the Medal of Honor since Congress authorized it in 1861. According to the Army, "Medals of Honor are awarded sparingly and are bestowed only to the bravest of the brave; and that courage must be well documented."

The upgrade from DSC to MOH has its own story, especially as MOHs are to be awarded within five years of the action involved. William Vollano, a retired social worker from Ann Arbor, interviewed Kettles as part of a Ypsilanti Rotary Club's Veterans History Project. Vollano had a wide-ranging discussion with Kettles and was winding up for the day when Kettles's wife Ann asked Charles to "talk about what happened on May 15."

On hearing the story, Vollano was convinced Kettles deserved the MOH, and worked with Kettles's son, Mike, to gather documents for review by the Defense Department and Congress. They received help from Michigan Congressman John Dingell and then from Congresswoman Debbie Dingell. A very long process ensued, including obtaining eyewitness accounts from personnel who were at the battle scene. Once receiving the Pentagon's approval, a one-time provision waived the five-year statute of limitations for such awards. In 2016, Kettles received this honor from President Barack Obama at the White House.

Charles Kettles spoke at the Yankee Air Museum in 2017 about the MOH mission. Kettles was not all that interested in all the fuss—in his view, the other pilots, gunners, and crew chiefs were equally as deserving of recognition for their service that day.

Kettles was far more than a war hero. He earned a master's degree at Eastern Michigan University (EMU), developing and teaching at the Aviation Management Program at EMU's College of Technology. One graduate, Delane Buttacavolli, is now a First Officer with Southwest Airlines and also volunteers as a pilot for the Yankee Air Museum's B-25.

EMU also hosts the Charles S. Kettles Veterans Resource Center and the Veterans Administration Hospital in Ann Arbor has been renamed in Kettles's honor. The Ypsilanti Historical Museum has a display about Kettles's life and many contributions.

Charles Kettles concluded his career at Chrysler Pentastar Aviation, retiring in 1993, and he passed away in January 2019. By all accounts, these three men—Albert, Richard, and Charles Kettles—had a great deal of humility about their remarkable aviation achievements and careers.

★ *Waco's original company name was sentence case "Waco." The updated aircraft are known as WACOs, in upper case.*

FOURTEEN

---◯---

Michigan and the
Strategic Air Command

"State of Michigan" B-52—courtesy of Wurtsmith Air Museum.

Michigan has been home for military air bases from the earliest days of the twentieth century. This chapter focuses on the three Michigan Strategic Air Command (SAC) Air Force Bases—Wurtsmith (in Oscoda), K.I. Sawyer (in Gwinn, south

of Marquette), and Kincheloe (in Kinross, south of Sault Ste. Marie).
All were used for defending the United States against the Soviet Union
during the Cold War and have now been repurposed for civilian use.

Before looking at the base histories, a light moment from the Cold
War is in order: In April 1959, Air Force Captain and Muskegon native
John Lappo flew his Boeing B-47 bomber under the Mackinac Bridge.
There is 155 feet of clearance between the underside of the bridge and
Lake Michigan/Huron; as a B-47 is 28 feet high, there was little room
to spare on this very high-risk escapade.

No problems occurred and there are no known photographs of this
episode. Lappo was court-martialed, fined, and grounded for the rest
of his Air Force career. He remained in the Air Force, receiving two
promotions, so he had rehabilitated his reputation.

Wurtsmith

Aviation roots in Oscoda began in 1923, when Loud Reames Field
opened. Named after World War I area aviators Harold Loud and Walter
Reames, the field was used by Selfridge Air Base aircraft, 200 miles to
the south. The Army Air Corps began flying aircraft to adjacent Van
Etten Lake, practicing wintertime landings on the frozen lake surface.
Winter conditions were difficult for flying—aviation gasoline was
hauled across the lake on sleds. Oil was heated in open fires before being
added to aircraft engines. Summertime usage included gunnery practice,
as there were fewer people and less boating activity than by Selfridge.

Residents raised $600 in 1924 to clear forty acres of land for the
base, as the local economy suffered from a serious 1911 fire. The field
was renamed in honor of Selfridge's Capt. Burt Skeel, who'd died in an
airplane crash that year. In 1942, Camp Skeel became Oscoda Army Air
Field. Assignments for base personnel included aerial protection of the
Sault Ste. Marie Locks and the Straits of Mackinac.

In 1943, several squadrons of the Tuskegee Airmen—African American aviators and ground crews—trained at Oscoda. Some of these men
were transferred from Selfridge, which struggled in dealing with racism
during World War II. One of their Commanding Officers was Benjamin
Davis, Jr., who became the Air Force's first African American general in
1954 on his promotion to Brigadier General.

Local political leadership was not receptive to having African American servicemen stationed in Oscoda. However, Michigan Governor Harry Kelly and Senators Homer Ferguson and Arthur Vandenburg all said this overt prejudice was indefensible; these men were fighting for America against a common enemy. Local residents were generally welcoming to these airmen, some of whom were housed by Gordon and Charlotte Welcome at the Welcome Hotel. Sgt. Burt Jackson wrote: "The men assigned to train at Oscoda are pleased that the only thing that is frigid is the weather, for the people of the region have been more than hospitable."

The base was renamed Oscoda Air Force Base in 1948 and was used in the filming the 1948 movie *Fighter Squadron* with Edmund O'Brien and Robert Stack. The base's name was changed again in 1953 to Wurtsmith Air Force Base. Detroit native Major General Paul Wurtsmith, who died in a 1946 airplane crash, had led the defense of Australian cities in World War II's early days against Japanese air attacks. His efforts were recognized by General Douglas MacArthur.

The base was used for fighter interceptor training in the early 1950s. New buildings and expanded runways were constructed to accommodate personnel growth and larger aircraft. The aircraft themselves became more sophisticated as technology advanced, such as the arrival of the supersonic McDonnell F-101 Voodoo in 1959.

SAC took over base jurisdiction in April 1960. SAC was an important element of the nation's defenses against the Soviet Union, with airfields throughout the country. Northern locations, such as Wurtsmith, were appealing as aircraft flying from these bases would have a shorter travel time to Soviet targets than from southern locations. Boeing B-52s began arriving on base and were a key element of U.S. defenses. B-52s were massive; each was powered by eight jet engines, weighed over 400,000 pounds fully loaded, and was capable of delivering either conventional or nuclear weapons almost anywhere in the world. The first B-52 on base was named the *State of Michigan*.

Other SAC-era aircraft on base included Boeing's KC-135 Stratotanker and Convair's F-106 Delta Dart. KC-135s were essentially gas stations with wings, providing mid-air refueling to SAC's bomber aircraft on long missions. F-106 fighters were part of the Air Defense Command network, protecting the continental United States. Among other armaments, F-106's could carry nuclear tipped antiaircraft missiles—a last line of defense if Soviet bombers broke through over the Artic.

Wurtsmith airmen were part of some of the most important military events of the twentieth century. The Cuban Missile Crisis in October 1962 was likely the closest the U.S. came to direct military conflict with the Soviet Union. The military was at Defense Readiness Condition 2, very close to nuclear war. Wurtsmith crews would have been part of any mission had events spiraled out of control.

Some personal stories add perspective to these events. Captain Dan Zahhos was a B-52 radar navigator stationed at Wurtsmith in 1962. Zahhos was relaxing in a bar and watching television after an October 1962 hunting trip, and remembered, "here comes the president (John Kennedy)" discussing the threat of nuclear missiles in Cuba. Zahhos drove to his parents' home in Minnesota, outlining evacuation plans if the situation further deteriorated. Recalled to Wurtsmith at 4:00 a.m. the next morning, Zahhos was on the road within thirty minutes for the 400-mile trip.

Wurtsmith housed bombers from Florida's Homestead AFB during the crisis, as B-52 crews based at southern U.S. airfields were redeployed north, out of Cuban tactical missile range. First Lieutenant Harold Andress said airplanes were parked "on every piece of concrete we had. Their alert crews bunked in the bachelor officers' quarters, the fire house, wherever...."

Airman Tom Hoover, who was nineteen at the time, remembered that leaves for Wurtsmith personnel were cancelled; everyone was working twelve-hour shifts, seven days a week. Hoover believed that virtually all personnel realized the world was at the brink of catastrophe.

Lieutenant (and later, Lt. General) E.G. Shuler, on alert with his B-52 crew at Carswell Air Force Base in Texas, described SAC's readiness for all bases: "We cocked every airplane we had...Everybody was target-studied. There were no training flights, no ground training, no nothing. We were ready to go to war."

President Kennedy and Soviet Premier Khrushchev were able to resolve the situation peacefully, but it was a very close call. However, conclusion of the Missile crisis did not end the Cold War. In the early 1960s, the Vietnam conflict was escalating and Wurtsmith crews participated extensively in Southeast Asia combat operations.

In 1965, some of Wurtsmith KC-135's were assigned to southeast Asia and began flying "Young Tiger" missions, mid-air refueling of bombers and fighters. Certain missions were never officially recorded as they occurred over enemy airspace. As this direct violation of standing orders saved the lives of American airmen, the practice may have been unofficially condoned.

1965 saw the beginning of "Arc Light" B-52 heavy bombing missions in Southeast Asia. Some crews were drawn from SAC's nuclear alert force, including Wurtsmith. B-52s flew over 126,000 sorties over Southeast Asia between 1965 and 1973. Vietnam's airfields were not long enough for B-52 operations, so these heavy bombing missions were flown from Guam, Thailand, and Okinawa.

Wurtsmith's B-52H models were not configured for conventional bombing, so crews received supplemental training on B-52D models that carried these weapons, before deploying to Southeast Asia. Arc Light concluded with "Linebacker II," an intense bombing of North Vietnam in December 1972 in which Wurtsmith airmen participated. This campaign, while controversial in the U.S., led to the January 1973 Paris Peace accords, concluding America's involvement in the Vietnam conflict.

The Cold War's risk of a surprise Soviet attack continued in the years after Vietnam. SAC bases would rotate aircrews on alert status—typically, twenty-four hours a day for a week—then the crews were on more normal hours the following two weeks. Airmen on alert status were housed in a complex near the runways nicknamed "the mole hole," a two-story building with offices and the mess hall upstairs and sleeping areas underground. Crews would live together and travel on base as a team, such as going to the base movie theater in an "Alert Vehicle." If the klaxon went off, crews would race to these vehicles and drive at high speed to their waiting aircraft, with other base traffic yielding the right of way. Aircraft taxiways looked like a "Christmas Tree" feeding into the main runway, facilitating quick take-offs.

Once alerted, the objective was to get airborne in fifteen minutes or less, and if ordered, fly to targets in the Soviet Union. Some F-106s would be airborne in five minutes or less ("Hot Birds"). These aircraft, with pilots and crew chiefs very close by, were fueled and armed and ready to take off.

There were many incongruities, such as the "Discovery Days" child care facility and nuclear weapons storage (sometimes referenced as the "bomb dump") being on the same base. And, when the klaxon sounded, crews might well have wonder: *is this a drill, or the end of the world?* And even if they survived the attack on the Soviet Union, what would they be coming home to?

As society changed, so did the military. The 1970s saw the first female B-52 crew chief in Air Force history, Sergeant Gail Pettigrew, at Wurtsmith. Crew chiefs had overall responsibility for aircraft maintenance, so theirs was a very visible, high-pressure job. Wurtsmith also had some of the first female Air Force security officers, including Sergeants Sonja Shuemake Pander and Regina Walker Maynard. Pander noted that once she established authority in her area of responsibility, few problems were encountered. Maynard observed that once base personnel saw she just wanted to do her job, same as everyone else, apprehensions about female security personnel largely disappeared.

Wurtsmith crews participated in Operation Desert Storm in January 1991. At the beginning of the conflict, crews flew about fourteen non-stop hours from Oscoda (with two in-flight refuelings), bombed targets in Iraq, and then landed at temporary bases in Saudi Arabia. Crews ultimately returned to their regular duties at Wurtsmith at the war's conclusion.

Combat missions were of course high-risk propositions, but any mission, for any purpose, had the risk of accidents and fatalities. In 1969, Major Robert Winn was able to return a B-52 to Wurtsmith when an engine pod fell off (the pod landed in an unpopulated area near the Au Sable River), then two additional engines had to be shut down. This incident may be the only instance of a B-52 landing with just four functioning engines. In September 1976, a KC-135 based at Sawyer AFB developed a mechanical problem and crashed on its way to Wurtsmith.

Five of the twenty personnel onboard survived. In an October 1988 incident, a KC-135 crashed in bad weather on landing approach to Wurtsmith. Six crewmembers lost their lives; ten other passengers and trainees were injured.

As the Cold War wound down, defense spending was under close scrutiny. In April 1991, a Base Realignment and Closure Commission recommended closing Wurtsmith, along with other U.S. bases. President George H.W. Bush and Congress approved this action. In December 1992, Wurtsmith's final B-52, the "Old Crow Express," departed; this aircraft is believed to have flown more missions than any other B-52 in Desert Storm.

Personnel assigned to Wurtsmith often had fond memories of their time on base and of the area. While some noted the cold winters, and the absence of dating prospects (the military had few women during the SAC years), many others have commented on lifelong friendships, as well as marriages that occurred from their time on base. Work skills and larger life lessons, acquired on base and in the Air Force, proved very beneficial when airmen returned to the civilian world. The Wurtsmith Air Museum, containing aircraft, exhibits, and displays commemorating nearly 100 years of aviation in Oscoda now occupies three former fighter alert hangers.

K.I. Sawyer AFB

The origins of SAC's presence in the Marquette area began with the establishment of K.I. Sawyer County Airport in 1949. The airport is in Gwinn, about twenty miles south of Marquette. Kenneth Ingalls Sawyer was a 1907 University of Michigan civil engineering graduate who became Marquette County's Highway Department Superintendent. He drafted much of Michigan's road legislation, instituted an early rural highway centerline marking program, championed plans for an area airport, and served as Ishpeming's mayor.

SAC's desire to have a wide geographic distribution of bases led to the 1955 signing of a lease between Marquette County and the Air Force for using the airport, and by 1957 all non-military operations had ended at Sawyer. Some of the first aircraft assigned to Sawyer

F-106 at the K.I. Sawyer Heritage Mission—courtesy of Lani Duquette.

were Convair F-102 Delta Daggers from Kincheloe AFB, which were temporarily stationed at Sawyer in 1958. 1960 saw the arrival of the first KC-135, which was christened *County of Marquette* (with a bottle of Lake Superior water), and the first B-52, *Pride of the Upper Peninsula,* arrived in 1961.

Also arriving in 1961 was the 56th Fight Group, part of the Air Defense Command system. The origin of the 56th goes back to World War II, when it was one of the best-known fighter groups in the 8th Air Force, credited with almost 1,000 enemy aircraft either shot down or destroyed on the ground.

Aircraft and personnel on base actively participated in many aspects of the nation's defense. Alan Miller was a Security Officer at Sawyer in October 1962. Shortly after President Kennedy's speech to the nation outlining the situation in Cuba, Miller was "summoned to the base's alert area where B-52s, loaded with nuclear bombs, were poised to strike upon the president's command. For the next six days, I donned combat fatigues, carried a sidearm, and worked the midnight shift overseeing the security of several bombers and KC-135 tankers." Miller was well aware the world was at the precipice.

Sawyer crews participated in "Operation Chrome Dome" missions, which kept a number of nuclear armed B-52s airborne at all times so, if the continental U.S. was attacked, these aircraft would have a head start on attacking Soviet targets. Then-Secretary of Defense Robert McNamara, reflecting the mindset of many military and political leaders, stated the U.S. and the Soviet Union should have "the capability of surviving a first strike and retaliating selectively," with the goal of providing a "more stable balance of terror."

In addition to Sawyer aircrews' service in Vietnam's Arc Light and Young Tiger missions and deployment to Iraq for Operations Desert Shield and Desert Storm, support was provided for civilian humanitarian missions, such as "Operation Sno Go" in late January 1977. Parts of western New York State and Pennsylvania were paralyzed in a severe blizzard—some areas had twenty-foot snow drifts. Crews from Dover Air Force Base flew into Sawyer (and other bases), then transported snow removal equipment and support personnel to the Buffalo, New York, Airport to assist with the clean-up effort.

As with Wurtsmith, the government decided to close Sawyer. That decision led to the founding of the K.I. Sawyer Heritage Museum in 1993 by Air Force Association Lake Superior Chapter 238. A home for the museum was located in 2005. A Vietnam veteran B-52 is on display at the museum, having been flown in by the Air Force in 1983. This aircraft, named *Black Bandit,* was damaged in Linebacker II operations over Vietnam, then was repaired and returned to operations.

The museum has an F-101 Voodoo, which is dedicated to the men and women of the 62nd Fighter Interceptor Squadron and to Sam Cohodas, a longtime banker and philanthropist in the area and a very active supporter of Sawyer AFB— a rare honor for a civilian.

One of the restoration projects the museum undertook was for an F-106, similar to those on base in the SAC years. Former Congressman Bart Stupak was instrumental in obtaining the aircraft and restoration began in 2005. A former Sawyer Crew Chief, Lani Duquette, was the Crew Chief and Project Manager for the F-106 work, leading a team of many dedicated volunteers was required. This aircraft was the ninth F-106 manufactured. It had been parked in the Air Force "boneyard" for twenty years in Arizona and was in rough shape. The museum team went to work, completing the restoration in 2006. Museum visitors now see a great looking aircraft.

The Marquette area was home to the aircrews and their families. Given the northern climate and typically heavy snowfall, some personnel referred to the base as "K. I. Siberia" (the Upper Peninsula's weather would be an adjustment for airmen from the south). That said, many personnel have fond memories of their time on base and of marriages, families, and friendships from their time at Sawyer, as well as of some non-military touches, such as picking blueberries from patches on base.

Kincheloe AFB

Military planners wanted to build an airfield near the Soo Locks given the importance of Great Lakes freight shipping. The airfield was built about twenty miles from the Locks and was originally designated Kinross Auxiliary Airfield. Kinross was a Sub-Base of Alpena Army Airfield and was a refueling stop for Alaska-bound aircraft as well as providing defense for the Locks. The base and airfield were leased to Sault Ste. Marie after World War II for private and commercial aviation.

As the Cold War intensified, the airfield was reactivated in 1952 and renamed Kinross Air Force Base. After the Air Force resumed control, the base was built up for fighter-interceptor operations. In 1959, Kinross was renamed Kincheloe Air Force Base in honor of Captain Iven Kincheloe, the first pilot to exceed 100,000 feet of altitude (reaching 126,200 feet in a Bell X-2). Born in Detroit, Kincheloe grew up in western Michigan and was a Korean War ace, downing five enemy aircraft.

B-52s began arriving at Kincheloe in 1961, after the runways were lengthened. Kincheloe-based B-52 crews flew on strategic "Operation Chrome Dome" missions—extremely long patrols loaded with nuclear weapons for a potential attack on enemy targets—as well as serving as heavy tactical bombers delivering tons of conventional, high-explosive ordinance during the Vietnam era's Arc Light and Linebacker II missions.

Iven Kincheloe grave, Arlington National Cemetery—Public Domain.

One Kincheloe crew was shot down on the night of December 26, 1972, after their B-52 was hit by Surface to Air Missiles (SAMs). Code named "Ebony 02," pilot Capt. Robert Morris Jr., and Electronic Warfare Office Maj. Nutter Wimbrow III were killed in the incident. Their bodies were returned home by North Vietnam in 1977. Crew members Capt. Michael Labeau (radar-navigator), TSgt. James Cook (gunner), 1st Lt. Robert Hudson (copilot), 1st Lt. Duane Vavroch (navigator), were captured and repatriated home in 1973.

Just before impact, Wimbrow saw the incoming SAMs on his display screen, calling to the crew on the intercom: "We're going to be hit." In a tragic irony, Morris' crew learned they would be flying that night while at breakfast that morning. Their table had a newspaper showing pictures of bomber crew members who had been lost a few nights before. After their meal, Morris and Wimbrow said they were going to get haircuts so they would "look good on Hanoi TV and in the papers tomorrow."

Back at Kincheloe, rumors of the shootdown began before official confirmation of what had happened. Staff Sergeant Keith Stanton, a B-52 Crew Chief, knew the Ebony-02 crew. Stanton noted the base was in a state of shock about the loss, with the war really hitting home. On his return home, Navigator Vavroch briefed Kincheloe personnel about the shootdown and about his time as a POW. The Ebony 02 crew was honored at a 2009 ceremony at Missouri's Whiteman Air Force Base (Morris was a Missouri native).

Kincheloe was also home for the 37th Air Defense Missile Squadron, which was equipped with BOMARC surface to air missiles. Designed and proven at the Willow Run facility in the mid-1950s, these were the first long-range anti-aircraft missiles in the world, and they could be armed with either conventional or nuclear warheads. The missile site was at Raco Army Airfield, about twenty miles from Kincheloe. "Raco" is from the Richardson and Avery Company, which operated an area sawmill in the nineteenth century. In World War II, Raco had been used for holding German POWs. The base was inactivated in July 1972.

Kincheloe AFB and the community had very close ties. For example, Chief Master Sergeant Joseph Durham opened the Durham Motor Inn near the back gate after his 1966 retirement from the Air Force. Durham had been a Crew Chief before retiring. The Inn was often used by airmen and their families new to the base before finding permanent housing. Daughter Susan Durham attended nearby Rudyard High School, along other students whose parents were stationed at Kincheloe. One memory that really stood out for Durham was hearing and seeing minimum interval takeoffs—where dozens of B-52s on ready alert status would take off a few seconds apart. This was a sight and sound that she will never forget.

The children of base personnel had a significant impact on the community. Rudyard (about nine miles away) provided education for middle school and high school students. Elementary age children attended school on base, and for a time that school had one of the largest student populations in Michigan. In a 2018 interview, Jim and Kathy Stenzel (involved in Upper Peninsula education) noted that "base" children were about 75 percent of the school enrollment. Children of base personnel might share their world travel experiences from where their parent(s) had been stationed with their local classmates, but most students seemed to get along well.

After the Bases Closed

Just as the SAC bases were an economic boom when they were active, the end of the Cold War and the ensuing base closures had an enormous economic impact. The Air Force tried to help. For example, General Rudolf Peksens was Sawyer's base commander as of the September 1995 closing. In the *Congressional Record* then-Congressman Stupak commented: "General Peksens was always there for the community, to give his advice, time, and assistance."

All three areas were economically hard hit with the closures. Each base had several thousand military personnel and supported hundreds of civilian jobs, and the base closings had a significant impact on schools, businesses, and local tax revenues. Community leaders in each area considered many alternatives for reviving their economies, such as establishing economic development commissions to attract businesses to the area and repurposing the air fields as civilian airports.

New technologies may help ease the economic pain. The Michigan Association of Manufacturers is planning on opening three space-related ventures over the next few years, focusing on low-orbit satellites. Marquette County will house a vertical (rocket) launch center. Oscoda will house a horizontal (take-offs and landing from a runway) launch center. The command center will be at Chippewa International Airport.

An ongoing concern is environmental contamination left behind by base operations Residents and on-base personnel have had serious health issue associated with this contamination. Clean-up efforts are very expensive, and many local residents are not satisfied with the remediation actions taken to date. Michigan's political leaders are involved, and while progress is being made, much remains to be done.

SAC's Role

Each of Michigan's three major SAC bases had a huge local impact and was a key part of winning the Cold War and in defending the United States. In 1984, Sgt. David Demmon, a B-52 tail gunner based at Sawyer, told an interviewer: "If the call came right now... I would have no qualms about flying off on a mission, even if it meant having to use nuclear weapons. I would be doing what the American people want me to do…I'd be helping to keep the peace."

The Wurtsmith portion of this chapter first appeared as "Wurtsmith Air Force Base —Past, Present, and Future" in *Michigan History,* a magazine published by the Historical Society of Michigan, Vol. 105 No. 1, January/February 2021 www.hsmichigan.org. Various edits have been made to the original article.

FIFTEEN

———————○———————

Some Good, Out of Tragedy

Michigan has had its share of military and civilian aviation tragedies. Taking to the skies always implies risk. The worst loss of life in Michigan aviation history occurred in August 1987, when Northwest Flight 255 departed from Detroit's Metro Airport heading for Phoenix. The McDonnell Douglas MD-82 did not generate sufficient lift on take-off due to pilot error, and 153 of the 154 passengers and crew on board and two people on the ground died.

This chapter focuses on three less-remembered air tragedies and shows how good can emerge, years later, from these nightmares. These events are the 1950 crash of Northwest Flight 2501, a 1971 crash of a Boeing B-52C Stratofortress (five miles from a nuclear power plant), and the crash if a University of Michigan charter jet with a cardiac transplant team on board in 2007.

Northwest Flight (NW) 2501

NW 2501, a twin-engine propeller powered DC-4, departed around 8:30 p.m. Eastern Standard Time on June 23, 1950 from New York City's LaGuardia Airport, heading for Seattle, with intermediate stops planned for Minneapolis and Spokane. On board were pilot Robert Lind, co-pilot Verne Wolfe, flight attendant Bonnie Feldman, and fifty-five passengers.

The flight encountered a severe storm over eastern Lake Michigan and crashed offshore shortly after midnight on June 24 between South

Haven and Benton Harbor. The exact location of the crash has never been determined, and the Civil Aeronautics Board (forerunner of the National Transportation Safety Board) investigated and could not conclude as to probable cause.

Former Northwest Chief Pilot Joseph Kimm was part of the accident investigation and believes turbulence was the likeliest reason for the crash. There also may have been incomplete communications from ground personnel with NW 2501 about the storm's path and severity.

A few witnesses close to the shoreline reported seeing or hearing a very low flying aircraft shortly before the crash occurred. There were no survivors and Coast Guard search efforts were unsuccessful. Some personal effects and unidentifiable human remains washed ashore, which were buried in two unmarked graves in Saint Joseph and South Haven. NW 2501 coverage was soon overshadowed by the Korean War's outbreak on June 25, 1950. As none of the fifty-eight deceased were from Michigan, local memory of the event has faded.

Years later, historian and underwater explorer Valerie Van Heest began investigating. Van Heest was a co-founder of the non-profit Michigan Shipwreck Research Association (MSRA), which had located several shipwrecks in Lake Michigan. An MSRA board member, Craig Rich, suggested searching for NW 2501. Rich's idea seemed impractical—no one knew exactly where this aircraft crashed, and it had been over fifty years since the accident. MSRA had limited funds and people, a short exploration season on the water, and initially decided not to undertake this project.

A fortuitous and totally unexpected phone call came in 2004. The late Clive Cussler, author and ship wreck explorer, called Rich in August 2004, offering assistance. Cussler would fund the use of his side scan sonar operator crew to work with MSRA in the search.

The first effort began in September 2004; these five days were unsuccessful, but Cussler offered to send his crew back the next spring and if needed in the future. The joint venture team located and documented ten new shipwrecks but had not found the crash site or any wreckage as of 2020.

Memorial Marker at South Haven, Photographer Tom Renner—courtesy of Valerie Van Heest.

MSRA took up the effort on their own in 2017 after Cussler stopped participating. The search has continued over 500 square miles of Lake Michigan. In Cussler's view "A wreck will be found only when it wants to be found" and given the results to date, it would be hard to dispute his conclusion.

Of course, finding the fuselage remnants would be only part of the story—far more important than the wreckage are the surviving family members. Families without closure sometimes have a harder time in dealing with the loss of a loved one than those who know what happened, an phenomenon sometimes described as "ambiguous loss." Closure may be limited without a body to properly bury. Those left behind may feel some irrational optimism (*Maybe the family member is stranded on an island?*) and then experience terrible despair when reality sets in.

In 2008, Van Heest presented the NW 2501 story at the Berrien County Historical Association. One of the attendees, Chriss Lyon, spoke with Van Heest afterwards. Lyon has background in genealogy, and her research offer was accepted and has proven very helpful in finding additional family members connected to the lost flight. Robert Cooley, a member of the Berrien County Genealogy Society, found there was an unmarked grave in St. Joseph's Riverview Cemetery. A note in the registry stated unidentified remains were buried on July 3, 1950 from a Lake Michigan aircraft crash.

Those remains had been handled by Louis Kerlikowske, who was Berrien County Coroner and a funeral home director at the time. Kerli-kowske donated a Riverview Cemetery plot, had the remains cremated, and placed them in an urn within the cemetery. This plot was unmarked until the registry notation was found, leading to a September 2008 memorial service facilitated by Van Heest.

The Riverview Cemetery now has a monument with the names of all fifty-eight of the deceased from the crash of NW 2501, which was donated by the Filbrandt funeral home. Robert Linstrom, then Pastor of South Haven's Peace Lutheran Church, officiated, remarking that: "We give thanks for the privilege of marking this place as hallowed ground…. In this hallowed place and in the grandeur of Lake Michigan's depths, the fifty-eight who died are entombed and we pause this day in reverent remembrance to commend them to God."

Van Heest spoke of honoring the memories of the deceased. Ken Skoug and Bill Kaufman took turns reading all fifty-eight names during the ceremony. Skoug's father and Kaufman's mother were lost on the flight. Many family members attended, one of whom wrote to Van Heest: "My sister Mary and I appreciate, more than words can ever express, all you and Mr. Cussler have done to help us know about the plane our grandparents and aunt were on." Another attendee noted his gratitude to Lyon for her work in reaching out to his family. Family members, as well as those who organized the service, likely found some measure of peace and serenity that day.

Van Heest's excellent book *Fatal Crossing* about the ongoing search efforts was published in 2013, and it seemed like matters had largely concluded. Time moved on; what more could be done?

Turns out, there was more—in a 2015 epilogue to *Fatal Crossing*, Van Heest described how she learned of a second unmarked grave in South Haven—thirty miles north of St. Joseph. Area resident Beverly Smith often placed flags at soldier's gravesites at South Haven's Lakeview Cemetery. Smith was researching cemetery records and found information indicating that remains believed to have been from NW 2501 crash victims were buried there in May 1951. Smith's great uncle, Joseph Bartunek, was one of the Coast Guard crew participating in search efforts for NW 2501.

Smith emailed Van Heest, who coordinated a second memorial service in June 2015—on the sixty-fifth anniversary of the crash. St. Joseph Monument Works donated and installed the rock used for this commemoration. Services were again led by Pastor Linstrom. This emotional scene had much the same result as the 2008 event—tears, memories, and trying to make sense of how life works.

The full story of the final moments of NW 2501 is not yet written. The likelihood is that, after seventy years, little identifiable wreckage remains and the mystery may never be solved. As of late 2020, however, Van Heest and the team are looking forward to the future. The word *quit* is not in anyone's vocabulary as searching for seventy-year-old wreckage requires patience. Honoring Clive Cussler's long-standing support and the desire of the family members to know what happened that night remain important goals.

B-52 over Charlevoix

Charlevoix's "Big Rock" ("Kitchiossining" to the Little Traverse Bay Band of Odawa Indians) is a boulder in Little Traverse Bay, not very far offshore and about five miles north of town. Local native tribes had used this location as a meeting place hundreds of years ago. Area visitors will now find a beautiful, peaceful scene, and they may not be aware of a 1971 Boeing B-52 Stratofortress crash in the Bay, which was a near-miss ecological disaster in which nine airmen were lost.

The crash had its roots in Consumers Power (now Consumers Energy) development of a nuclear power plant in the area. Local residents had been assured that sufficient safety protocols were in place. Construction began in July 1960 and the facility was completed in October 1962.

Big Rock was Michigan's first commercial nuclear power plant and was used for research, electricity generation, and producing cobalt 60 as a by-product for treating cancer. A promotional spot narrated by Ronald Reagan was filmed touting Big Rock and nuclear power. The location became a tourist attraction with the 500,000th visitor arriving in 1968.

As nuclear plants were coming online, the United States was at the height of the Cold War with the Soviet Union. An integral part of U.S. deterrence was the Strategic Air Command (SAC), which heavily relied on long-range B-52s, bombers capable of delivering nuclear weapons anywhere in the world. U.S.-based squadrons routinely carried out training missions to maintain readiness. B-52s had been developed for high-altitude flights as there was little risk of being shot down. By the late 1950s improved Soviet air defense capabilities had placed high altitude B-52s at risk. In response SAC altered its tactics and redesigned training missions for altitudes of 700 feet or less when the bombers neared their "target."

Big Rock was appealing for practice missions as it simulated one of the expected targets in any future conflict with the Soviet Union. In 1963, SAC moved the 1st Combat Evaluation Group Detachment 6 from

Ironwood to Bayshore, a small town between Petoskey and Charlevoix. Detachment 6 conducted Radar Bomb Scoring (RBS), evaluating B-52 crew effectiveness by using radar pulses to simulate bomb drops. The RBS facility had about 100 personnel with no food service or housing onsite. Personnel lived in the local communities, with Charlevoix High School providing the airmen Saturday morning use of the gym.

During a flight, the RBS site and the B-52 crew would be in radio communication. When the B-52 was ready to acquire its target, the crew initiated a series of electronic pulses. The pulses allowed tracking of the aircraft's course and estimating where its "bomb" would have hit. The B52s also practiced overcoming electronic countermeasures from the RBS location.

One of the corridors used by SAC for low altitude bomber flight routes was over Lake Michigan. Since the era's jet engines were not very efficient at low altitudes, smoke trails behind the aircraft led to the flight paths becoming known as Oil Burner (OB) routes. OB-9 was the Lake Michigan route, with B-52s flying in a corridor about eight miles wide, often directly over Big Rock Point.

People on the ground had concerns about overflights so close to the new nuclear plant. A November 1963 letter from the Atomic Energy Commission's Director of Regulation to the Air Force noted, "It has come to our attention that the Strategic Air Command has been using the Big Rock Point Nuclear Power Plant at Charlevoix, Michigan, as a target for practice bombing runs" and then asking to have flights rerouted because of the risk. In December 1967, a Consumers Power employee was "concerned about using Big Rock as a practice target" and the risk of a bomber crash into the plant.

Consumers Power communicated their concerns several times, such as a 1970 letter to Michigan Congressman Gerald Ford, who was then the U.S. House of Representatives Minority Leader. Less than three weeks before the crash, Ford wrote the Air Force in late December "concerning the low altitude high speed training route used...which passed directly over the Big Rock Point Nuclear plant...the power company is particularly concerned...because its insurance company has just increased the annual premium on the (plant)."

Another factor leading to the tragedy was SAC's usage of older B-52C models for U.S.-based practice missions. Newer B-52s were in Southeast Asia for the Vietnam War or on nuclear deterrence assignments. Many of the older B-52Cs had extensive flight hours, and all were attached to Westover Air Force Base, near Springfield, Massachusetts.

All this set the stage for the January 7, 1971 tragedy. Mission briefing had taken place the day before at Westover. Code named Hiram One Six, the nine-member crew would fly the OB-9 route. After completing the bombing simulation, Hiram One Six would return to Westover.

Mission commander was Lt. Colonel William Lemmon, an experienced pilot with an outstanding reputation. The evaluating instructor described Lemmon as an "excellent [pilot] in all areas...very professional as an aircraft commander." Background information suggests all nine crewmen served in Vietnam before assignment to Westover, so Hiram One Six was in the hands of a very experienced group of flyers.

Hiram One Six took off shortly before 2:00 p.m. (Eastern), heading to northern Lake Michigan. Other than a minor hydraulics problem, no mechanical issues were reported during the flight. Once near Michigan, the crew descended into the low-level OB-9 flight route.

Northern Lake Michigan weather that day was typical for January, with light snowfall. The crew had four simulated targets, with Big Rock being code named CHARLIE. Hiram One Six successfully "bombed" the first three targets and was lining up "CHARLIE," when radar operators at Bay Shore RBS observed a light burst on their screen and lost all contact with the crew. No distress signal was received. At the same time, a tremendous explosion and fireball burst over Little Traverse Bay around 6:30 p.m.—about six miles from the RBS site and five miles directly north of the nuclear plant.

Local residents had witnessed the sky light up and heard the explosion. Herbert Cummings stated it was the largest fireball he'd ever seen. Mrs. Virgil Haynes was leaving her home in the area, heard a terrific explosion, and said "the scene was like that of a sunset.... the entire sky was lighted up." Staff Sergeant Harry Gibbs, stationed at Detachment 6, was off duty that night and was outside his home shoveling snow. Hearing the explosion, he and a neighbor drove to the shoreline—the

Memorial near Charlevoix—courtesy of the author.

fire made them think a freighter had exploded. Inside the RBS, Airman First Class Daniel Smith was on duty, and he reported that the team that night initially thought there was a communication equipment malfunction.

The explosion prompted an intensive search by the U.S. Coast Guard. Crew members were not located and were declared dead several days later. Only small amounts of debris was recovered in the initial search. The Air Force Accident Investigation Board led the investigation, with assistance from the U.S. Navy Supervisor of Salvage and Ocean Systems, a private firm in Florida. The Coast Guard Cutter *Mackinaw,* now on display at Mackinaw City, also participated.

According to the official U.S. Navy salvage report, the wreckage covered an area about 2,400 yards by 1,600 yards in water over 200 feet deep. Some wreckage was retrieved in the two weeks following the crash, but a late January blizzard struck the area and the search was called off until spring 1971. At that time, Ocean Systems retrieved aircraft parts including engines, crew compartments, tail and wing sections, and landing gear and wheels. All recovered items were taken to Kincheloe Air Force Base near Sault Ste. Marie and laid out in a hangar for inspection.

Boeing and Air Force personnel's analysis concluded the accident was a result of structural failure between the left wing's two engine pods—each wing of a B-52 has two engine pods, and each pod has two engines. The sudden, catastrophic loss of the wing resulted in the B-52 becoming unflyable and crashing into the water. The brilliant explosion reported by witnesses had resulted from the large amount of highly flammable fuel on board, much of which was stored in the aircraft's wings. No human remains were ever recovered. The aircraft had been used past its serviceable time with metal fatigue causing the wing failure. SAC reviewed the findings and ordered the retirement of all remaining B-52Cs from service.

After the crash, citizens began asking "what if the nuclear plant was hit?" Political activist Ralph Nader wrote a letter to the AEC, stating "what is difficult to understand is why flights had not been suspended earlier...it is symptomatic of the federal bureaucracy that no action was taken on these requests until a plane actually crashed."

Big Rock released a statement addressing the risk of the reactor being compromised. The statement noted that factors such as the weight and velocity of the object hitting the plant and the strength of the reactor's containment sphere would determine if radioactive materials would be released into the environment. When asked if the plant could sustain a hit from very large, heavy aircraft such as a B-52, a spokesman responded, "we think so, but this is speculation." Given the weight of a B-52 and the presumed high speed at impact, this conclusion seems optimistic.

Further analysis suggested that emergency shutdown mechanisms used in the nuclear plants would not work well enough to prevent catastrophe, which may have taken the form of a radioactive cloud being released. Some scientists thought such a cloud could be lethal up to 100 miles from the point of origin.

Years later, a 2011 incident suggested what could have happened if Big Rock's reactor was compromised. A tsunami disabled the power supply and cooling of Japan's Fukushima reactors, causing a nuclear core meltdown. As a result, there were mass evacuations of the local population. While radiation deaths from this disaster are unknown, some people may have died from the stress of forced evacuations. A small number of residents returned to the Fukushima area in 2019, suggesting that if the worst had happened, Charlevoix would have had a difficult and slow recovery.

The Air Force suspended flights over Little Traverse Bay until an assessment of crash probabilities was delivered to Consumers Power. The April 1971 "risk analysis" and subsequent review resulted in a compromise: low level training exercises would continue with a wider range around the plant than on the fatal flight. Modified B-52 flights continued until 1984 when Bayshore RBS closed.

While the local area was spared a nuclear accident, there were nine airmen on the flight of Hiram One Six who lost their lives. Crew members were Lt. Colonels Lemmon and John Simonfy, Jr., Majors Donald Rousseau and Gerald Black, Captains John Weaver and Joel Hirsh, 1st Lieutenants Douglas Bachman and Dennis Ferguson, and Technical Sergeant Jerry Achey. These men left behind nine widows and seventeen children.

Memorial services were held at Westover AFB and then, in July 1971, in Charlevoix to honor the crew. A B-52 flew over Charlevoix followed by a formation of F-106 aircraft in the missing man formation. After the crash, there were rumors in the area that hydrogen bombs remained in the Bay. Five years before the crash of Hiram One Six a 1966 midair collision over Spain involving a B-52 had resulted in three hydrogen bombs landing in a village and one in the Mediterranean Sea. Hiram One Six did not carry any bombs on its training flight, but it is easy to see how the rumors started.

Forty years later a rededication ceremony, organized by area historian Richard Wiles, took place at Lake Michigan Shore Roadside Park, south of the crash site. Wiles searched for surviving family members before the ceremony, and the widow and two daughters of Major Rousseau attended.

The ceremony included comments by Wiles and the Rousseau family, an invocation by a local pastor, a three-volley salute by an honor guard, and a bugler playing taps. Joanne Rousseau Pollock (Major Rosseau's widow) commented "Don had such a great spirit and love of life…(he was) committed to doing the best he could. We remember, love and honor him and the other eight men lost to us with this ceremony today."

During the Rousseau's visit, a thunderstorm occurred while the area near the memorial still had clear weather. The family quickly returned to the memorial and, as hoped for, saw a beautiful rainbow over the Bay, which was likely both an emotional and soothing moment.

Based on remarks at the time and later comments by the Rousseau family, Wiles clearly did a good deed toward helping family members obtain closure. The Air Force had provided little information to the families about the incident, and Wiles's research bridged the gap.

As the country's appetite for nuclear power diminished, Big Rock Point was rechristened Big Rock Point Restoration Project and decommissioning work began in 1997. Spent nuclear fuel was put into temporary on-site storage, pending shipment to a permanent nuclear waste storage facility. Plans for permanent storage have not been finalized and eight canisters of nuclear waste remain on-site, stored under twenty-four-hour security. Presumably, most area residents would prefer that the dangerous spent fuel be shipped away, but finding a location willing to take this material is not easy and shipping the fuel has its own risks, so the final resolution of the Big Rock Point reactor is unclear.

A small marker with the names of the deceased was installed on one of the boulders and is maintained by Greenwood Cemetery of Petoskey. Family and friends of the Hiram One Six crew will never forget the tragic events of January 7, 1971. Their lives have been impacted ever since. The one saving grace of that terrible accident is how fortunate the Charlevoix area was on that sad night.

University of Michigan Health System

Thirty-six years later, tragedy struck again in Lake Michigan. On June 4, 2007, a Survival Flight jet with four University of Michigan Health System (UMHS) professionals and two Marlin Air pilots (a charter air service used by the University for such flights) crashed into Lake Michigan shortly after take-off from Milwaukee, Wisconsin, with the loss of all onboard. The aircraft was a twin-engine jet Cessna Citation 550.

The crew and medical team were returning to Ann Arbor after surgically obtaining lungs for a transplant patient. (UMHS was able to procure another set of lungs after the crash.) Team members lost on the flight were David Ashburn, a cardiothoracic fellow; Richard Chenault II, and Rick LaPensee, transplant donation specialists; and Martin Spoor, a cardiac surgeon and U-M faculty member. The Marlin Air pilots were Bill Serra and Dennis Hoyes.

U-M staff were "shaken to the core" in the words of an ICU nurse on duty that night—the medical professionals on the flight were well known and highly respected. To have this sort of tragedy occur on a lifesaving mission was incomprehensible then and remains so now.

The National Transportation Safety Board (NTSB) evaluated possible explanations for control issues reported by the pilots shortly after takeoff. The NTSB found the two explanations that were most consistent with what was known about the crash—either an inadvertent autopilot engagement or a runaway electric pitch trim. As the available evidence both supported and contradicted these scenarios, the NTSB could not go further in its analysis. Additional analyses of the causes are included in the NTSB's report; an extensive list of recommendations was developed to avoid similar tragedies in the future.

As one might expect, U-M honored their team.

Artist Doug Hollis designed and erected a sculpture outside the University's Hospital in memory of the transplant team. Hollis, an Ann Arbor native and University of Michigan alumnus, described the piece as a "kinetic screen," which appears to be moving liquid when there is any sort of wind. Located outside of the hospital's main entrance near the "Flight for Life" helipad, the "Rotations" sculpture is made of stainless steel and contains 450 moving components.

Hollis was selected to create the work by a university task force several years after the accident. He initially noted he typically did not create this kind of work, but with the passage of time, the selection team and family members were open to a non-traditional memorial.

Hospital visitors will find a small, peaceful garden by the memorial and portraits of those lost inside the hospital lobby. Several scholarship funds have been endowed in the names of the deceased. While the

Rotations sculpture, U-M Hospital—courtesy of the author.

tributes and scholarships are wonderful memorials, the deceased left behind families, some with young children, and all of the survivors are likely dealing to be with this emotional trauma for years after the crash.

Organization such as Ele's Place could help with the aftermath. Founded in 1991, Ele's Place was created by the work of Betsy and Woody Stover, whose daughter, Helen Louise (nicknamed "Ele") had passed away at eleven months old, as well as by mental health professionals. The Stover's were coping with both their own grief as well as that of their other young children. It was clear that children and teens facing these circumstances would benefit from having support services available.

In 2007, Ele's Place opened in an Ann Arbor church. Martin Spoor's widow, Susan Torrible, brought her three young children to Ele's place. This church did not have sufficient space to meet the needs of all of the attendees; unfortunately, life's misfortunes ensures a constant need for these support groups.

Fast forward to 2019: Ele's Place moved into a new facility in Ann Arbor, after a successful fundraising campaign supported by Torrible, other individuals, and local corporations. Several million dollars were received in corporate and private contributions, reflecting the community's commitment to support grieving children and families. The new facility includes the Martin Spoor Library, with over 160 children participating weekly in Ele's Place programs prior to the coronavirus situation.

Meanwhile, life moved on for families and friends of the crash victims. Susan Torrible, a physician by training, has channeled her considerable talents into photography, specializing in photos of military veterans. She is updating a website highlighting these veterans—not for commercial purposes, but to honor the service of these men and women to their country.

She describes her motivation in her words:

My real creative passion is taking photographs of people who are in their senior years…the elders of our communities, (including) photos of aging veterans—those men and women who served in World War II, Korea and Vietnam. Their stories and their photos are important to listen to and look at, and I am honored every time I take these photos to learn, listen and capture an image of our important history.

Presumably, nearly everyone reading these words has dealt with loss and tragedy in their lives. No doubt, it is a very personal matter in how one deals with such things, which may take years to resolve internally. It is good to know the healing process can appear at unexpected times and unexpected ways.

The B-52/Charlevoix part of this chapter first appeared as "'A B-52 Tragedy: Charlevoix's Near Miss with Nuclear Disaster" in *Chronicle,* a magazine published by the Historical Society of Michigan, Vol. 44 No. 1, Spring 2021 www.hsmichigan.org. Various edits have been made to the original article.

SIXTEEN

○

Michigan Aviation Hall of Fame

Edsel Ford, 1937 Senate Hearing—Library of Congress, Prints & Photographs Division, photograph by Harris & Ewing, [reproduction number, e.g., LC-USZ62-123456]

Established in 1987, the Michigan Aviation Hall of Fame (MAHOF) honors the men and women who have made significant contributions to our state's aviation history. Some of these people are Michigan natives, while others have come through our state at different points in their aviation careers. All of these pioneers have left their mark. This book has only described a cross-section of these individuals—some of whom appear in multiple chapters as their contributions span many years in various roles.

MAHOF was originally located in the R.E. Olds Transportation Museum in Lansing. Bob Ellis, then-President of the Air Zoo Air & Space Museum visited the Olds Museum and initiated a chain of events regarding the future home of MAHOF. Ellis met with one of MAHOF's founders and then-President Herb Swan, who had his own distinguished career in Michigan aviation. Swan and the Lansing group were at one point considering building a MAHOF structure at Lansing's Capital City Airport. The ensuing discussions between Ellis, Swan, and the respective Boards resulted in the move to the Air Zoo.

MAHOF's website has biographical sketches of all of the enshrinees, which are well worth reading. The individuals listed below are all MAHOF enshrinees as of March 2021 and either contributed to and/or were written about in this book. I have had the privilege to read about all of them and to have met several of them.

Talbert "Ted" Abrams	Albert Kettles	Col. Preston "Pete" Parish, USMC
Prof. Harm Buning	Lt. Col. Charles Kettles, USA	Suzanne Parish
Lt. Cdr. Roger Chaffee, USN	Lt. Col. Alexander "Jeff" Jefferson, USA	Ann Pellegreno
Urban "Ben" Drew	Clarence "Kelly" Johnson	Edward "Eddie" Rickenbacker
John Ellis III	Capt. Iven Kincheloe, USAF	Eddie Stinson

Robert Ellis	Dr. Richard Light	William Stout
Edsel Ford	Brig. Gen. Charles Lindbergh, USAF	Herbert Swan
Henry Ford	Capt. Jerry Linenger, USN	Col. Alfred Worden, USAF
Col. Francis "Gabby" Gabreski, USAF	Neal Loving	Irving Woodhams, Sr.
Capt. Ralph "Randy" Hotton, USN	Col. Jack Lousma, USMC	Maj. Gen. Paul Wurtsmith, USAF
Col. Raymond Hunter, USAF	Brig. Gen. James McDivitt, USAF	
Conrad "Connie" Kalitta	Dennis Norton	

Bibliography

Books

Abbott, Ace, *Rogue Aviator*, Auburn, New York: Allen Morris Publishing, 2015.

Abrams, Ted, *Essentials of Aerial Surveying and Photo Interpretation*, Johnson City, Tennessee, Johnson Press, 2008

Bak, Richard, *Detroitland*, Detroit, Michigan: Painted Turtle Press, 2001.

Beld, Gordon G., *The Early Days of Aviation in Grand Rapids*, Cheltenham, England: The History Press, 2012.

Baime, A. J., *Arsenal of Democracy*, Boston, Massachusetts: Mariner Books 2015.

Bluth, John, *Stinson Aircraft Company*, Mt. Pleasant, South Carolina: Arcadia Publishing, 2002.

Brinkley, Douglas, *Wheels for The World*, New York, N.Y.: Penguin Books, 2004.

Brown, Barbara Burt, *The Abrams Family of America*, Rockland, Maine: Picton Press, 2008.

Burgess, Colin and Doolan, Kate, *Fallen Astronauts—Heroes Who Died Reaching for the Moon*, Lincoln, Nebraska: University of Nebraska Press, 2013.

Cole, Wendy, *Women Pilots of World War II*, Salt Lake City, Utah: University of Utah Press, 1992.

151

Cumming, William, *Iron Mountain Ford Motor Company Plant, Kingsford, Michigan, 1920-1951* [author must complete facts of publication]

Gubert, Betty Kaplan, Sawyer, Miriam, Fannin, Caroline, *Distinguished African Americans in Space,* Portsmith, New Hampshire: Greenwood Press, 2001.

Hanson, Victor Davis, *The Second World Wars,* New York, N.Y.: Basic Books, 2017.

Heaton, Dan, *Forgotten Aviator, The Byron Q. Jones Story,* Wellesley Massachusetts: Branden Books, 2012.

Homan, Lynn and Reilly, Thomas, *Black Knights—The Story of the Tuskegee Airmen,* New York, N.Y.: Pelican, 2002.

Hotton, Randy and Davis, Michael, *Willow Run,* Mt. Pleasant, South Carolina: Arcadia Publishing, 2016.

Hyde, Charles, *Arsenal of Democracy,* Detroit, Michigan: Wayne State University Press, 2013.

Loving, Neal, *Loving's Love—A Black American's Experience in Aviation,* Washington, D.C.: Smithsonian Press, 1994.

Mason, Dan, *History of Metro Airport,* Mt. Pleasant, South Carolina: Arcadia Publishing, 2011.

Maurer, Maurer, *Aviation in the U.S. Army, 1919–1939,* Forest Grove, Oregon: University Press of the Pacific, 2004.

McCarthy, James and Allison, George, *LINEBACKER II— A View from the Rock,* CreateSpace Independent Publishing, 2012.

Nigro, Lou and Larsen, Deb, *Selfridge Air Field,* Mt. Pleasant, South Carolina: Arcadia Publishing, 2006.

O' Callaghan, Tim, *The Aviation Legacy of Henry and Edsel Ford,* Detroit, Michigan: Wayne State University Press, 2002.

Parish, Suzanne, *Suzanne Parish Memoirs,* Upjohn, Delano, Parish Trust, 2012.

Travis, Bill, *Pan Am Captain, Aiming High (and PAN AM series First Airline Pilot Job Interview),* Gilbert, Arizona: Trabidi Publishing, 2013.

Van Heest, Valerie, *Fatal Crossing,* Holland, Michigan: In-Depth Editions, 2013.

Weiss, David – *Saga of the Tin Goose, the Story of the Ford Tri-Motor,* Holly, Michigan: Cumberland Enterprises, 2006.

Other sources

Towler, Tommy (editor), *We Were Crewdogs, Vol VIII.* Amazon Kindle edition.

Silent Wings, *American Glider Pilots in World War II (2007 documentary).*

The Congressional Record, Volume 141, Issue 72.

Willow Run Reference Book, compiled by the Plant Guide Staff, Feb. 1, 1945

Haulman, Daniel, *The United States Air Force and Humanitarian Airlift Operations 1947–1994,* Maxwell AFB: Air Force Historical Research Agency, 2012.

Oral History of the Willow Run Rosies: Marge Haskins, Jean Zaranko, Michigan Oral History Association.

Magazines

Air & Space, Air Classics, Aviation History, Popular Mechanics, Michigan History, Michigan Historical Review, American Surveyor, Nuclear News, Flypast, Air Force, Warbirds International. Air Line Pilot, Warbirds Digest.

Newspapers

Ann Arbor News, Canton Observer, Capital News (Lansing), Charlevoix Courier, China Press (English version), Detroit Free Press, Detroit News Easton (Maryland), Star Democrat, Lansing State Journal, Grand Rapids Press Greenville Daily News, Iron Mountain Daily News, Kalamazoo Gazette, Ludington Daily News, Mt. Clemens Monitor, The Mining Journal, New York Times, Petoskey News Review, The Press of Atlantic City, San Francisco Chronicle, The Sault News, Selfridge Field News

Special thanks

I have had the very good fortune to have the support of Emily Allison at the Historical Society of Michigan and Chuck Springston and Carl Von Wodkte at HistoryNet in developing stories and allowing me to share previously published works. Also, Lori Martinsek at Adept Content Solutions has been extremely helpful over many months in getting the project pulled together.

Interviews and email correspondence

Michigan's aviation history covers decades, in all parts of the state. Help from many people in researching this story was absolutely essential. The contributions and the selfless commitment of these people have been enormous—so, thank you very much, and my apologies to anyone I have inadvertently omitted:

Alison Beatty, Barb Christensen, Bette Kenward, Bill Cummings, Bob Bailey, Bob Ellis, Boyd Naylor, Chriss Lyon, Christy Kincaid, Chuck Shuler, Claire Dahl, Dan Smith, Dave Barnhart, Dave Callanan, Dave Pequet, Dave Powell, David Thompson, Dennis Norton, Don Kettles, Duane Zantop, Sr., Elizabeth Workman, Greg Ward, Harry Friedman

Harry Gibbs, Jeannette Gutierrez, Jennifer Rousseau, Jim Redick, Jr., Joanne Pollock, Joe Amend, Joe Mazzara, Joe Provost, Judy Gager, Judy Shuler, Julie Osborne, Keith Stanton, Kevin Walsh, Kyle Abbott, Lance Kuhn, Lani Duquette, Lori Nye, Luke Noble, Lynn Beatty, Maggie Morris

Matt Anderson, Matthew Zavilij, Michael Dow, Nick Consiglio, Norm Ellickson, Paul Hakala, Phil Handleman, Randy Hotton, Ray Hunter, Richard Wiles, Shane Patzer, Shirley Balinski, Susan Durham, Susan Torrible, Tom Hoover, Valerie Van Heest, Wayne Fetty, Wendy Zielen, Wolfgang Franke

Archives

Benson Ford Research Center, Dearborn
Bentley Historical Library, Ann Arbor
Charlevoix Historical Society, Charlevoix
Fighting Falcon Museum and Flat River Museum, Greenville
Frankenmuth Military Museum, Frankenmuth
Greenwood Cemetery, Petoskey
Iron Mountain Museum, Iron Mountain
Kalamazoo Air Zoo/Michigan Aviation Hall of Fame, Portage
Mt. Clemens Library, Mt. Clemens
Northville Historical Society, Northville

Selfridge Air Base (including historical summaries by Dan Heaton), Harrison Twp.

Wright State University Archives and DaytonInnovationLegacy.Org, Dayton Ohio

Yankee Air Museum Archives, Belleville

Ypsilanti Historical Society, Ypsilanti

Facebook Groups

Some are dedicated to preserving the memory of different organizations and their members can offer great insights to history. Groups visited include: Willow Run—Ford's Army Air Force Plant #31, Zantop International Airlines, Westover AFB, Bayshore RBS, Wurtsmith AFB, Kincheloe AFB, Rudyard Michigan Hometown, National Stinson Club, K. I. Sawyer AFB, and Wurtsmith Air Museum.

Thank you all very much.

Made in United States
North Haven, CT
07 December 2021

12123066R00098